Philosophy is at once the most sublime and the most trivial of human pursuits.   (William James, *Pragmatism*)

I do not think that pragmatism has a True Self.
(Richard Rorty, *Philosophy and Social Hope*)

CONTENTS

PREFACE

Strictly, 'New Pragmatism' is a descriptive phrase itching to become a name. I have given it capital letters to help it on its way. But, this does not mean that this book is oddly premature: professing to provide an introduction to a currently non-existent movement. There is plenty for a fledgling name to latch on to.

The great American pragmatist revivalist Richard Rorty used the phrase 'New Pragmatism' occasionally, and in descriptive senses that matched our own purposes (e.g. 2000a: 95). He wanted to stake out a philosophical position that derives from the original pragmatism of William James and John Dewey,[1] but differs in two main aspects. First, it avoids talking about experience, along with empiricist notions in general, by talking about language instead. And secondly, it abandons the idea that there is such an epistemically sweet thing as scientific method, something that should serve as a model for all enquiry, because whoever practises it maximizes their likelihood of attaining true beliefs.

Cheryl Misak (2007) recently relied on 'New Pragmatists' as the title of a very worthwhile anthology of writings by thinkers who, despite her own anti-Rortyan predilections, mostly fit in with our broader aims. They are linked to the pragmatism of Charles Sanders Peirce, William James and John Dewey in various ways, and with varying degrees of tightness. Moreover, their approach to philosophy manifests three fairly straightforward pragmatist commitments: (i) objectivity is "historically situated", and none the worse for that, (ii) "knowledge has no foundations", and (iii) philosophy needs to keep "connected to first order inquiry, to real examples, to real life experience" (*ibid.*: 6–7).

In this book, we interpret the 'New Pragmatism' differently in a manner that goes beyond what either Rorty or Misak was disposed to say. We add a number of characteristics. Some of these make it somewhat clearer as to how practitioners of the New Pragmatism are related to the original pragmatists (we call them 'classic pragmatists') while at the same time showing how they differ from other philosophers, including other contemporary pragmatists and fellow travellers.

We introduce the New Pragmatism to help readers identify, and play off against one another, members of a useful cluster of philosophical views that promise both intellectual and social hope for the future. There is an additional hope, embedded within the whole fabric of the book, that those who find themselves attracted to the philosophical outlook it describes will find it easier to further their own correlative ambitions and communicate about them with kindred spirits if they can gather together, metaphorically or otherwise, under a single banner.

Certainly, the New Pragmatism will have done intellectual culture a terminological favour if it nudges aside the label 'neo-pragmatism', one that even Rorty was prone to using from time to time. The prefix 'neo', as in 'neo-Freudianism', 'neo-Marxism' and 'neo-liberalism', almost always carries connotations of substandardness, as if the version in question is not quite the real thing. This book is premised on the sincere assumption that the New Pragmatism is anything but that.

Finally, a brief word about the introductory nature of this book. Philosophers are fond of saying that philosophy has no shallow end. That is certainly true. But, it is nothing to either boast about or apologise for. And it does not mark out anything special about philosophy. Try diving into an introductory text on pure mathematics, corporate finance, literary theory or, indeed, any subject around which a substantial body of literature and critical thought has been built; unless you are already familiar with some of the background material, you will soon find the water flowing over your head. Having said that, this book aims to reach an audience of non-specialists without lapsing into condescension and yet without making the waters of exposition run so shallow that philosophers themselves cannot swim in it. This difficult task has necessitated some trade-offs.

On the one hand, to save space and keep up the pace, thinkers and philosophical views have been introduced rather swiftly at times, without stopping to explain their meaning and significance to the uninitiated. This should not pose an insuperable obstacle to such readers, although they may feel momentarily uncomfortable with the resulting holes in their comprehension. Sometimes context will eventually fill these, sometimes a footnote or a bit of extra thinking will do the trick, and sometimes something that is said later might help. Furthermore, there is advice at the end of the book in the section entitled "Reading the New Pragmatists" on where to find out more about who or what appears to have been precipitously introduced in the main text (e.g. W. V. Quine or Donald Davidson and their respective views). There is, however, also a sense of purpose behind the swiftness.

This book is designed to encourage readers to move on to explore New Pragmatist thinking. And for that reason, it does not dwell on matters that should be signposted for narrative purposes but need not be explored. It does not, for instance, go into detail regarding the traditional philosophical problems concerning the relationship between mind and body, the necessary and sufficient conditions for knowledge and so forth. These are problems that New Pragmatists wish to ignore and would, moreover, like to see either bypassed or dropped. They do not believe philosophy is like inoculation. There is no need to inject readers with a dose of its problems in order for them to be able to avoid them in future.

On the other hand, philosophically literate readers are likely to feel frustrated by the failure to provide greater technical detail on certain philosophical claims or to push certain lines of argument further. They no doubt seek the provision of a more sophisticated line of pragmatist thought. There are currently some very accomplished and imaginative thinkers working with pragmatist ideas who do just that in spades. They include Robert Brandom, Bjørn Ramberg and Roberto Unger, as well as those contributing to Misak's collection. This is not the place to deal with their complex and finely tuned work. However, for those who want to see what the New Pragmatism is like when it steps up another gear or two – perhaps by developing "a Rortyan post-ontological case for the distinctiveness of agency" (Ramberg 2000), explicating "Wittgenstein's pragmatism about norms" (Brandom 1994), or radicalizing some strands of pragmatist thought for current political purposes (Unger 2009) – there is also some special purpose bibliographical guidance for 'experts' in "Reading the New Pragmatists".

ACKNOWLEDGEMENTS

I owe Steven Gerrard, Kate Williams and the rest of the Acumen team a great debt of thanks for their exemplary patience and professionalism in steering this book through to publication. I would also like to thank my whole family, but especially Lesley, Jannie and Sophie, for their support and encouragement. Thanks are due also to Professor Anton van Niekerk along with my other colleagues at Stellenbosch University for their kindness in making me feel welcome and at home in a new intellectual environment. Emma Bell and Stephen Mullan provided characteristically perceptive comments on an earlier draft that led to some useful improvements. I am extremely grateful to them both. An anonymous reviewer also made a number of apt suggestions.

Finally, I should record my immense gratitude to all those scholars who have worked so hard and imaginatively over so many years, often against the tide and in other intellectually unfavourable circumstances, to foster a receptive intellectual environment for pragmatist approaches to philosophy. If the New Pragmatism continues to succeed on the terms outlined in this book, it will owe much to all of them.

Alan Malachowski
Arabella Country Estate
South Africa

ABBREVIATIONS

CIS   *Contingency, Irony, and Solidarity* (Rorty 1989).

DE   *Democracy and Education* (Dewey 1916).

EN   *Experience and Nature* (Dewey 1958).

ERP   *Essays in Radical Empiricism* (James1996)

EWO   *Ethics without Ontology* (Putnam 2004).

LW   *The Collected Works of John Dewey: The Later Works* (Dewey 1981–2008).

PMN   *Philosophy and the Mirror of Nature* (Rorty 1979).

PMT   *Pragmatism and The Meaning of Truth* (James 1998).

POQ   *Pragmatism: An Open Question* (Putnam 1995a).

PWP   *Philosophical Writings of Peirce* (Peirce 1955).

RP   *Reconstruction in Philosophy* (Dewey 1920).

1
INTRODUCING
THE NEW PRAGMATISM

There is absolutely nothing new in the pragmatic method.
(William James, *Pragmatism and The Meaning of Truth*)

Pragmatism, when looked at in wide perspective and against the background of earlier epochs of philosophic thought, is justified in thinking of itself as 'a new way of thinking'.
(Milton K. Munitz, *Contemporary Analytic Philosophy*)

The aim of this book is to provide a broad-based introduction to the New Pragmatism for those who are to a large extent, or perhaps even completely, unfamiliar with it. In tackling that task, it ranges over five large questions: what is the New Pragmatism? Why has it come into prominence in recent years? What, if anything, is *new* about it? What are its main strengths? And what are its prospects?

In dealing with such big questions, the book cannot help but evoke further issues. Some of these are subsidiary, and hence disposable. Others are quite important. However, most of the latter, especially those involving complex matters of history and textual interpretation, cannot be dealt with in the space available. And the others simply have little relevance to an introductory project of this kind. Furthermore, the overarching goal here is to cut through such complexities in order to provide a clear, accessible, general guide to the New Pragmatism, one that explains what it involves in the most general sense, why it has created such an intellectual stir in many quarters[1] and what makes it so interesting and challenging at the present time.

Notwithstanding its avowed introductory status, the book may also be of some interest to those who regard themselves as familiar, perhaps all too familiar, with the kind of pragmatism it describes. For the relationship between the New Pragmatism and its historical ancestor is often misunderstood, and this generates confusion and faulty lines of criticism. In setting the record straight, the book may encourage some victims of such misunderstanding to view the New Pragmatism in a different light, and to reconsider its potential.

The general structure

This short opening chapter outlines the structure of the book as a whole. It then goes on to discuss, in preparatory terms, what is meant by the label the 'New Pragmatism'. In doing so, it goes beyond the brief terminological justification given in the Preface and sets the scene for the more explicit treatment of the topic provided towards the end of Chapter 2.

That chapter fills in some background concerning classic pragmatism. This was the original form of pragmatism. It was given birth to by the writings of the American philosopher Charles Sanders Peirce. But it only began to make significant impact in the hands of two other famous American thinkers: William James and John Dewey. We do not discuss classic pragmatism in any depth. Just enough historical detail is furnished to flesh out an informative contrast with the New Pragmatism. For we need to show what it is that the New Pragmatism is trying to leave behind, why it finds it necessary to part company in this way, and why it makes consistent sense to say that the New Pragmatism is both historically rooted and something of a fresh departure. This material will perhaps provide additional insight into why the work of some New Pragmatists has provoked such harsh criticism from many of those who nevertheless remain attracted to pragmatism itself.

Building on the account offered in these preliminary remarks, Chapter 2 argues that a number of main features distinguish the New Pragmatism from its venerable ancestor. It contends that these features in particular also help mark it out as something new. Some of these are worth flagging now. In the first place, the New Pragmatism is resolutely 'cosmopolitan'. It has lost, in Giles Gunn's suitably evocative phrase, its "American colouration" (1995: 298) and thereby shaken off the provincial image that dogged classic pragmatism for so long.[2] It is now thereby able to exert a stronger influence across borders, both academic and geographical.[3] The second feature is 'autonomy'. The New Pragmatism has largely broken free of the analytic tradition that trapped its predecessor in unending, and largely fruitless, disputes. For this reason, the New Pragmatism has been able to start fashioning its own agenda and is liable to continue doing so in ways that are currently unpredictable. Its proponents do not generally waste much time engaging with the kind of tradition-bound criticisms of classic pragmatism that were once believed to be compelling. This is a controversial matter because some such criticisms remain in currency and are still considered unanswerable. The final feature can be tagged 'neoteric'. It concerns the way in which the New Pragmatism has updated the philosophical approach of its predecessor and become more attuned to the present-day ethos. It is not, for example, enamoured with science or wedded to certain empiricist notions that prevented adherents of classic pragmatism from adapting it to take advantage of useful developments in both philosophy itself and the wider intellectual tradition. Among these developments, the so-called 'linguistic turn', when philosophy began to focus on language as a means of clarifying, if not dissolving its problems, is the most important.

Chapters 3 and 4 deal, consecutively, with the two philosophers who have done by far the most to develop, inspire and promote the New Pragmatism. The first is Richard Rorty, who taught for extended periods at Princeton University and the University of Virginia before moving to Stanford University where he was highly productive until his death in 2007. And, the second is Hilary Putnam, who has stayed at Harvard University throughout his lengthy philosophical career and is now Emeritus Professor there. Many other thinkers have paved the way for the recent revival of interest in pragmatism. These include Richard Bernstein, Susan Haack, Robert Westbrook, Richard Shusterman, Nicholas Rescher, Christopher Hookway and Cheryl Misak, whom we mentioned in the Preface.[4] However, it is Rorty and Putnam who have been most responsible for the ascendance of the

New Pragmatism itself. For that reason, and to clarify the nature of the very different contributions that they have made in this respect, their work dominates many of our discussions and most of these pages.

Chapter 5 identifies some of the key differences between the ways in which these two major thinkers approach pragmatism, then assesses the implications of such differences for the New Pragmatism. It concludes that the New Pragmatism can flourish on the input of both Rorty and Putnam without needing to reconcile *all* their differences. However, it also contends that other thinkers with fresh ideas will need to come forward to carry the New Pragmatism on to the next stage. Only then will it begin to fulfil the potential envisaged by its recent advocates.

Chapter 6 starts by quickly recalling some common objections to the New Pragmatism. Since this is an introductory account, no attempt is made to explore these or provide detailed arguments in the New Pragmatism's defence. However, by then it should already be clear that in many cases such arguments are unnecessary because these objections are often outdated or now tend to miss the point for other reasons.

Critics who voice the objections in question fall into two camps. There are those who argue that the New Pragmatism has found itself in much philosophical trouble because it has strayed from the path of classic pragmatism. Here, Peirce is often invoked as the path-maker, and founding father of pragmatism proper, a person of scientific rectitude and logical rigour whose principles have since been harshly betrayed. Others contend that the New Pragmatism does not hold water precisely because it is still, despite some catchy cosmetic changes, a form of *pragmatism* and thus vulnerable to certain basic objections that were voiced, or so it is claimed, with great clarity and force long ago by critics such as G. E. Moore and Bertrand Russell. In keeping with our theme 'it is time to move on', we do not investigate these criticisms in any depth. But, to give an indication, and some assurance, as to why this is not required, we outline Putnam's objections to Russell's treatment of James in Chapter 4.

A third camp should be mentioned. Its members also reject the New Pragmatism because it resembles classic pragmatism. But, they are equally opposed to the early critics of classic pragmatism. For they are practitioners of continental philosophy who take their bearings from such thinkers as G. W. F. Hegel, Friedrich Nietzsche and Martin Heidegger, thinkers they regard as standing apart from, if not in opposition to, the Western Platonic tradition. This is a bankrupt tradition that, in their eyes, classic pragmatism colluded with even when appearing to dispute it. The third camp's attitude is briefly discussed in the chapter on Rorty, a philosopher who daringly and provocatively attempted a pragmatist appropriation of some of the very thinkers who are deemed to separate the continental approach from Platonism and its alleged co-conspirators.

The book finishes with a general discussion of the future prospects for the New Pragmatism. These prospects are themselves mainly pragmatic. They cannot be properly assessed independently of the New Pragmatism's burgeoning relationships with diverse disciplines including literature, law, education, feminism, politics and religion. For although it has achieved a large measure of *philosophical* autonomy in the sense just mentioned, and later explained in more detail in Chapter 2, the New Pragmatism derives much of its intellectual vitality and practical utility from its various connections with other forms of thought and cultural expression. Indeed, the verdict of the primary concluding argument is that the New Pragmatism has the best chance of consolidating its recent progress if it continues to engage imaginatively with ideas outside the traditional spheres of philosophy. To do this will require plenty of skill, imagination and perseverance. For advocates of the New Pragmatism must manage to steer past the Sirens of classic pragmatism who beckon them towards a nostalgic, but now hopelessly irredeemable, past and those of postmodernism who seek to serenade them away from their more serious social hopes and political ambitions. The New Pragmatism has the best chance of staying on course if it makes the most of the intellectual freedom it has carved out for itself and then, to borrow a thought from Coleridge that Rorty liked to recall, helps create the standards of taste by which it is to be properly judged.

The whole project is rounded off with "Reading the New Pragmatists", a short bibliographical essay. This offers some suggestions for the kind of further reading that encourages deeper exploration of the various issues raised at a more preparatory level throughout the book. In that sense at least it helps plug some of the gaps that necessarily occur in an introductory text.

What is the New Pragmatism?

At first sight, the question is thoroughly unpragmatic. Its form replicates that of the great Socratic questions invoked by the Platonic dialogues: what is X?[5] These questions seduced a whole tradition of Western philosophizing into elevating 'theory' over 'practice'. It thereby embarked on a seemingly endless quest for the elusive 'necessary and sufficient conditions' supposedly required to put such persistently troublesome queries to rest. Nevertheless, our question can be posed in a suitably pragmatic way if we use it merely to probe for some very general practical features: those that will help us identify the kind of things that a New Pragmatist is liable to assert, to be interested in, to oppose and to write about.

When the celebrated American philosopher W. V. Quine surveyed pragmatism's relationship to empiricism, he wittily suggested that the term "pragmatism" may be one "we can do without" because "it draws a pragmatic blank" (1981: 3). However, there was still a hint of the Socratic approach even in Quine's pithy ploy. For it places too much emphasis on the idea of locating a 'pragmatic criterion' – one without which a word, phrase, distinction, claim or whatever is surplus to philosophical requirements – almost as if, without the quest for 'necessary and sufficient conditions', there would have to be some *other* quest because some *other* criterial hole would have to be filled. By contrast, the New Pragmatism circumvents all such concerns. It relies, instead, on a family of more practical considerations. These include whether something is useful, whether it engages our interests, whether it helps us cope in the appropriate circumstances, whether it helps us make better sense of the world around us, and, more generally, whether, following James's lead, it fits in with our already secured fund of beliefs and experience. The New Pragmatism does not seek to provide a substitute for the Socratic problematic, but rather tries to show how we can live comfortably without it. If we substitute 'non-practical' for 'non-empirical', the following quotation from Dewey captures what it is that New Pragmatists generally try to avoid here: "The problems to which non-empirical method gives rise in philosophy are blocks to inquiry, blind alleys; they are puzzles rather than problems" (EN: 6). And James famously provided a graphic example of how practical concerns can be invoked to put to rest disputes that can otherwise seem interminable:

> Some years ago, being with a camping party in the mountains, I returned from a solitary ramble to find everyone engaged in a ferocious metaphysical dispute. The *corpus* of the dispute was a squirrel – a live squirrel supposed to be clinging to one side of a tree-trunk; while over against the tree's opposite side a human being was imagined to stand. This human witness tries to get sight of the squirrel by moving rapidly round the tree, but no matter how fast he goes, the squirrel moves as fast in the opposite direction, and always keeps the tree between himself and the man, so that never a glimpse of him is caught. The resultant metaphysical problem now is this: *Does the man go round the squirrel or not?* He goes round the tree, sure enough, and the squirrel is on the tree, but does he go round the squirrel? In the unlimited leisure of the wilderness, discussion had been worn threadbare. Everyone had taken sides, and was obstinate; and the numbers on both sides were even ... "Which party is right," I said, "depends on what you *practically mean* by 'going round' the squirrel. If you mean passing from the north of him to the east, then to the south, then to the west, and then to the north of him again, obviously the man does go round him, for he occupies these successive positions. But if on the contrary you mean being first in front of him, then on the right of him, then behind him, then on his left, and finally in front of him again, it is quite obvious that the man fails to go round him, for by the compensating movements the squirrel makes, he keeps his belly turned towards the man all the time, and his back turned away. Make the distinction [i.e. between these two practical senses of the phrase 'going round'], and there is no occasion for any further dispute". (PMT: 27–8)

New Pragmatists take from this kind of example exactly the kind of lesson that James did. Philosophical disputes that may appear to be intractable are best tackled by trying to identify the respective practical consequences of the different viewpoints at stake and then making distinctions accordingly. But, as we shall see, they do not try to work this lesson up into a full-blooded methodology. New Pragmatists consider James's own references to the 'pragmatic method' to be unnecessary encumbrances on what is a very useful starting-point in dealing with philosophical issues.

Pragmatism over postmodernism

Pragmatism represents the break-up of cultural and religious authority, the turn away from any simple or stable definition of truth, the shift from totalizing systems and unified narratives to a more fragmented plurality of perspectives.
(Morris Dickstein, *The Revival of Pragmatism*)

So, to return to our original question, what is the New Pragmatism? At first glance, it is a form of philosophy that shares many of the characteristics associated with postmodern philosophy in general. Bernd Magnus (1995: 213–14) has profitably listed these as follows:

1. A putative anti/post-epistemological standpoint (one that avoids giving priority to the study, and establishment, of the nature of knowledge);
2. antiessentialism (opposition to the assumption that certain things have properties that can be identified as constitutive of their identity);
3. anti-realism (the idea that there is a way things really are, independently of any of our conceptions of them, is regarded as disposable or incoherent);
4. opposition to transcendental arguments and viewpoints;
5. rejection of the picture of knowledge as accurate representation;
6. rejection of truth as correspondence to reality;
7. rejection of final vocabularies (denial that certain words have the final philosophical say on important matters);
8. rejection of canonical descriptions (any description can be improved upon or replaced by one more useful or otherwise appropriate);
9. denial that any of the above characteristics implies relativism, scepticism or nihilism;

10. suspicion of grand narratives or meta-narratives;
11. rejection of the 'metaphysics of presence' (this is difficult to pin down independently of the complex role it plays in the thought of Heidegger and Jacques Derrida – it involves rejection of any notion we can conceive of some pure 'presence' of a thing that is not contaminated by anything outside itself [examples include: an instant of time isolated from the past and future or a self that has no sociohistorical entanglements]);
12. rejection of the typical binary oppositions that tend to play a constitutive role in philosophical thinking (e.g. mind–body, and fact–value);
13. rejection of the notion of the neutrality and sovereignty of reason (and a recognition of its gendered, historical and ethnocentric features);
14. a conception of 'world–world' mappings as social constructions;
15. historicism;
16. dissolution of the concept of the autonomous, rational subject;
17. ambivalence towards the Enlightment and its ideology;
18. rejection of standard accounts of the division of labour in knowledge acquisition and production.

There are two things to establish: the relevance of postmodernism and the fact that, despite the overt similarities, the New Pragmatism is distinguishable from it.

Postmodernism is relevant because it characterizes much of the intellectual ethos of the developed West. Even if you have never heard of it, you are likely to have been influenced in your thinking and general outlook by some of the points listed above.[6] The jargon, which you may not recognize, is irrelevant. When discussing any significant issue, you are liable to be sensitive to such things as the possibility that there are different viewpoints on the matter that cannot be subsumed under a single position without controversy and the necessity of taking into account any bias or distortion of the facts caused by considerations of gender, race or cultural background. Postmodernism raises these concerns. Furthermore, many of the above points have seeped through into popular culture in disguise where, even when they are lampooned, they exert an intellectual influence.[7]

Although it blends in with the prevailing ethos,[8] the New Pragmatism differs from postmodernism in at least two senses:

(a) The New Pragmatists tend to repudiate some of the listed characteristics of postmodernism. Here, (3) and (17) in particular stand out, but (6) also needs to be treated with some reservation.
(b) The motivation for assuming many of the characteristics listed above is different. It comes from the work of James, Dewey and other thinkers sympathetic to classic pragmatism rather than the writings of key figures within the tradition of continental philosophy, who have generally been hostile or, at best, indifferent towards pragmatism in any case (e.g. Heidegger, Michel Foucault and Derrida).[9]

Repudiating some basic tenets of postmodernism

Postmodernism fosters an intellectual attitude best captured by Rorty's memorable term 'knowingness'.[10] Its proponents tend to look down on those who subscribe to any form of realism or believe that the Enlightenment bequeathed to us a valuable set of general principles for underpinning intellectual enquiry. The New Pragmatism holds that such accusations of naivety in this respect are themselves naive: that its own down-to-earth outlook trumps the contrived, condescending knowingness of postmodernism. In the case of 'realism', Rorty, for example, argued that the philosophical issues involved have a historical rather than metaphysical basis and that once this is revealed, once the roots of the images and metaphors that lend them credence are dug up, they become optional. He contended that it is then best simply to dispense with such issues. Continued consideration is likely to yield nothing of practical value. To deal with them by taking an anti-realist stance, thereby substituting anti-realist terms for realist ones, or kicking up some other big rhetorical fuss, is to keep a fruitless dialectic in play.

The New Pragmatism occupies an intellectual space outside the whole realist–anti-realist debate.[11] In Chapter 4, we shall see that Putnam adduces different reasons for distinguishing pragmatism and anti-realism. He maintains that, despite appearances, the classic pragmatists, and James in particular, were not anti-realists. However, although Putnam's approach attributes realism to James, it provides further support for the New Pragmatist view that the *philosophical* opposition between realism and anti-realism is spurious: that what needs to be said in realist terms can be said in ordinary language games – games that require no metaphysical (or anti-metaphysical, for that matter) grounding. In Chapter 5 we outline why Putnam's position does not need to be aligned with Rorty's.

The New Pragmatism finds the Enlightenment questionable, but only to the extent that its original spirit of independent, fair-minded enquiry has been solidified into cumbersome, large-scale, universal methodologies, principles and theories. Rorty regarded the New Pragmatism as remaining faithful to that original spirit: as keeping enquiry free and open while being prepared to honour and live by the results even as they are considered to be subject to revision. And Putnam reinforces the New Pragmatism's reservations about the Enlightenment by positing the need for an additional 'Third Enlightenment', a pragmatist Enlightenment. This Enlightenment avoids the ossification of methodology, principle and theory by instead 'valorizing' what Putnam calls "reflective transcendence" (EWO: 96). Such 'transcendence' invokes the capacity to stand back and evaluate our customary beliefs and practices without using a realist metaphysics as a point of reference. It involves what Dewey called "criticism of criticisms" (quoted in *ibid.*),[12] where the resources employed do not require special philosophical support. The community of enquiry finesses its practices of enquiry from within even as it attempts to rise above itself in terms of self-improvement.

Postmodernists are inclined to reject the notion of truth as correspondence to reality. The New Pragmatists agree that the notion is a regrettable one, but only as a *deep explanatory* notion. James regarded the thought that beliefs are true because they correspond to how things are in reality as a platitude, as something of little philosophical value or significance. The New Pragmatists are with him on this. What they object to is the further thought that 'correspondence' can be taken out of its banal context and worked up into a theory that gives us insights regarding the more profound nature of truth, insights that transcend the social practices that justify its conferral in particular cases. In Chapters 3 and 4, we take a closer look at how

Rorty and Putnam prepared the ground for the New Pragmatism's view of correspondence.

Motivation

Our reference to motivation as a distinguishing mark of the New Pragmatism serves two purposes. First, it provides a quick example of New Pragmatist thinking. And secondly, it helps us to mark out further differences, this time between the New Pragmatism and classic pragmatism.

In the tradition that the New Pragmatism wants us to break out of, it is usually considered wrong-headed to make direct inferences about the truth of beliefs on the basis of their origins. Someone who does so commits the so-called genetic fallacy. Against this, the New Pragmatism holds that stories about how beliefs come about can have some bearing on how their truth should be assessed. For, as James vehemently argued, once the notion of 'bare correspondence' is recognized to be idle for serious explanatory purposes, a host of factors can be profitably consulted to determine truth.

The contention that the New Pragmatism should be distinguished from postmodernism on the basis of the motivation for its adherence to certain views that postmodernism shares is an example of genetic or 'genealogical' thinking. Such thinking results from the New Pragmatism's shaking up of the kaleidoscope of orthodox philosophical notions in the interests of making philosophy more productive, more interesting and more useful. In this case, 'origins' have some definite practical consequences. If we started to unpack the characteristics and commitments on Magnus's list, we would find that they take on a different aspect when the inspiration behind them is classic pragmatism. Some examples of this 'unpacking' will be evident throughout the book. Meanwhile, it is important to note that in seeking to change the philosophical landscape, the New Pragmatist tries hard to avoid the kinds of moves that shaped the old one. Thus it would be a mistake to assume that simply because it holds that accounts of origins *can* play a role in truth assessment, the New Pragmatism is attempting to somehow *reduce* truth to a matter of origins.

The New Pragmatists have been inspired to shift into new territory by the writings of the classic pragmatists rather than those of the, seemingly more radical, representatives of continental philosophy. And 'inspired' is an important term in this context. For the word encapsulates another important distinguishing feature of the New Pragmatism.

It regards James and Dewey in particular as inspirational figures rather than purveyors of all-purpose doctrine or methodology.[13] When James gave his famous characterization of a pragmatist as someone who "turns his back resolutely and once for all upon a lot of inveterate habits dear to philosophers" (PMT: 31), he was voicing the kinds of words that would later inspire those open to the idea that pragmatism could be revived in a new shape. For James recommended turning away from "abstraction and insufficiency, from verbal solutions, from bad *a priori* reasons, from fixed principles, closed systems, and pretended absolutes and origins" (*ibid.*). This list of philosophical deficiencies is echoed by the disenchantment that Rorty voiced in his groundbreaking book *Philosophy and the Mirror of Nature* (which we discuss in Chapter 3). Although he said surprisingly little of an explicit nature about pragmatism in *that* book, Rorty was already busy making intellectual culture more receptive to the idea that the writings of James and Dewey were well worth a fresh examination, and that they could not only enkindle a new form of pragmatism, but give philosophy itself a new, and more interesting, lease of life (see e.g. Rorty 1982).

However, the pragmatism Rorty envisaged – what we here call the 'New Pragmatism', differs from its progenitor in being much more flexible about doctrine and methodology. Although, for example, it endorses classic pragmatism's *practical* approach to philosophy, one that speaks to complex and diverse experiences of how life is actually lived, it does not attempt to articulate fixed definitions and principles that underpin that endorsement. Hence a New Pragmatist may well invoke James's and Dewey's conversational tendencies to elevate concrete practical matters of fact and experience over abstract theoretical considerations in passages such as these:

The pragmatist clings to facts and concreteness, observes truth at work in its particular cases, and generalizes.   (PMT: 17)

It is astonishing to see how many philosophical disputes collapse into insignificance the moment you subject them to this simple test of tracing a concrete consequence. There can *be* no difference anywhere that does not *make* a difference elsewhere – no difference in abstract truth that doesn't express itself in a difference in conduct consequent upon that fact, imposed on somebody, somehow, somewhen. The whole function of philosophy ought to be to find out what definite difference it will make to you and me, at definite instants of our life, if this world formula or that world formula be the true one.

(*Ibid*.: 30)

There is, I think, a first-rate test of any philosophy which is offered to us: Does it end in conclusions which, when they are referred back to ordinary life-experiences and their predicaments, render them more significant, more luminous to us, and make our dealings with them more fruitful? (EN: 7)

However, he or she has no time for formal enshrinements of such philosophical sentiments, tending to regard Peirce's famous attempts to formulate 'pragmatic principles', and the subsequent debates over counter-examples to them, to be a waste of time.

The New Pragmatists are inclined to view classic pragmatism as a rough and ready, but luminary, source of guidance rather than a reservoir of detailed maps. They believe any such maps will now fail in new terrain. For these are liable to depict too many old-fashioned quarrels with pragmatism's early critics and rely on outmoded conceptions of experience and science. Later, the various ways in which the New Pragmatism has created its own identity on the basis of such illuminative guidance will become clearer.

A curious unrest

In 1904, James vividly described circumstances that he felt were very likely to make the 'younger generation' in particular more receptive to fresh ways of thinking:

It is difficult not to notice a curious unrest in the philosophic atmosphere of the time, a loosening of old landmarks, a softening of opinions, a mutual borrowing from one another on the part of systems anciently closed, and an interest in new suggestions, however vague, as if the one thing sure were the inadequacy of extant school solutions. The dissatisfaction with these seems due for the most part to a feeling that they are too abstract and academic. Life is confused and superabundant, and what the younger generation appears to crave is more of the temperament of life in its philosophy, even though it were at some cost of logical rigor and purity.   (ERP: 39)[14]

In a sense, James was speaking too soon. The 'curious unrest' that he refers to was not quietened at the time by the kind of philosophizing he advocated. Instead, the Frege–Russell–Wittgenstein revolution in analytic philosophy was unleashed, and this quickly squashed any craving for "the temperament of life … at some cost of logical rigor and purity". In doing so, it relegated pragmatism to the sidelines. However, had James been speaking like this more recently, say in the last quarter of the twentieth century, he would have identified some of the factors that made the intellectual world more responsive to a revival of interest in his writings on pragmatism.[15] By then, the revolution in analytic philosophy had itself generated some of the unrest and dissatisfaction James earlier depicted.

These circumstances played a key role in the birth of the New Pragmatism. But, the right people needed to be on hand to make the most of them. Rorty and Putnam turned out to fit the bill. Rorty identified serious grounds for being disillusioned about "the inadequacy of extant school solutions". These, or so he argued, depended on dubious presuppositions that were blind to their own historical origins and yielded little of current practical value. Furthermore, Rorty claimed to have identified a self-undermining 'dialectic' within analytic philosophy itself, one that, in his eyes, highlighted a need to make way for something different:

I hope to convince the reader that the dialectic within Analytic philosophy, which has carried philosophy of mind from Broad to Smart, philosophy of language from Frege to Davidson,

15

epistemology from Russell to Sellars, and philosophy of science from Carnap to Kuhn, needs to be carried a few steps further.

(PMN: 7)

At more or less the same time, Putnam was also becoming increasingly dissatisfied with the prevailing tradition, and for similar reasons. But, his remedy was more conservative. Rorty wanted philosophy to move on to new ground, following some of the general directions given by Dewey and James. Putnam, by contrast, wanted to retrieve what was useful from classic pragmatism and graft it on to the existing tradition in those places where it would fit most beneficially.[16]

We should not, however, exaggerate the role that argumentation has played in preparing the ground for the New Pragmatism. Rorty and Putnam have been influential in the latter respect not just on account of their arguments in favour of a pragmatist approach to philosophy but also, to put it bluntly, because of who they are. Both made significant contributions to analytic philosophy before their pragmatist turn.[17] This means that the New Pragmatism gained considerable impetus from a sort of 'philosophical celebrity' effect. In the first place, on a theoretical level, the views on pragmatism that Rorty and Putnam voiced were at least taken more seriously because they were the views of two distinguished and highly respected thinkers. In addition, such views also attracted attention because they were the views of 'insiders': philosophers who were familiar with the details of the tradition they criticized and had proved their mettle within it.[18] And, finally, on the practical front, these well-known philosophers changed the intellectual climate in such a way that those who found pragmatism congenial were better able to get funding for publishing projects, conferences, new journals and so forth. Suddenly, a biography of Dewey, a conference on the relationship between James's radical empiricism and his pragmatism, a thesis on feminism and early pragmatist thought and other such ventures that would have probably seemed quite futile[19] a decade or so earlier, began to look like good ideas. The shelves in libraries and bookshops started to fill up with works devoted to pragmatist themes. Rorty and Putnam were largely responsible for this.

2

LEAVING CLASSIC PRAGMATISM BEHIND

The whole function of philosophy ought to be to find the characteristic influences which you and I would undergo at a determinate moment in our lives, if one or other formula of the universe were true.

(William James, *Pragmatism and The Meaning of Truth*)

The precise details of the early history of 'classic pragmatism' are still disputed.[1] Nevertheless, it is quite clear who the key figures were.

There were three of them. Charles Sanders Peirce was the founder in the sense of coining pragmatism's name and some of the main ideas first associated with it. But, according to John Murphy (1990: 33), it was William James who first used the designator 'pragmatism' in print. He extended the scope of Peirce's ideas, and attracted much greater attention to pragmatism in doing so. When he linked up with a keen ally in America, John Dewey, pragmatism was launched as a fully fledged philosophical movement.

Belief in action: Peirce

On his own account (PWP: 269–71), Peirce was prompted to conceive of pragmatism as a distinctive approach to philosophy by discussions that took place between him and a group of "young men in Old Cambridge" who began meeting together in 1872 and called themselves, "half ironically, half defiantly, 'The Metaphysical Club'". The members included James, Francis Ellingwood Abbot, John Fiske, Nicholas St John Green, Oliver Wendell Holmes, Joseph Bangs Warner and Chauncey Wright. Of these, Peirce mentioned St John Green as being particularly notable because "he often urged the importance of applying Bain's definition of belief as 'that upon which a man is prepared to act'". Peirce further claimed that, on his own conception of it, pragmatism was "scarce more than a corollary of" this (*ibid.*: 270).

Presumably, he afforded Alexander Bain's definition such great importance because it dovetailed with what he considered to be the key feature of pragmatism: an emphasis on practical concerns.[2] Indeed, this seems to come out clearly in the draft of a letter Peirce addressed to the editor of a newspaper: "The particular point that was made by Bain, and that had most struck Green, and, through him, the rest of us, was the insistence that what a man *really believes* is what he would be ready *to act upon*, and to risk much upon" (PWP: 325, emphasis added). Peirce's most significant contribution to classic pragmatism was to provide an initial formulation of what this emphasis on the practical amounted to, along with a general explanation as to its philosophical significance. The formulation came in the shape of what James would later refer to as "the principle of Peirce, the principle of pragmatism" (PMT: 29). This was delineated in an article entitled "How to Make our Ideas Clear": "Consider what effects, that might conceivably have practical bearings, we conceive the object of our conception to have. Then our conception of these effects is the whole of our conception of the object" (PWP: 31).

Looking back on his initial attempts to expound pragmatism, Peirce later explained the purpose of trying to identify the "practical bearings" of our conceptions of things more clearly than he had in earlier writings. He claimed that attempting to do this better enables us to determine whether the words we use to describe how we think of things are genuinely meaningful. But these were not to be just any old words: "Pragmatism is, in itself, no doctrine of metaphysics, no attempt to determine any truth of things. It is merely a method of ascertaining the meanings of hard words and abstract concepts" (*ibid.*: 271).

This was not, however, an early anticipation of analytic philosophy's famous linguistic turn, which occurred when it started to claim that philosophical problems could not be resolved without attending to the difficulties caused by the language in which they were couched. Although Peirce spent much time discussing linguistic considerations, he tended not to differentiate sharply concepts and ideas. Nor was he always careful, or even perhaps inclined, to distinguish either of these from the words used to express them. Hence it is not surprising that when he expanded on what "hard words and abstract concepts" are, he said he understood pragmatism to be "A method of ascertaining the meanings, not of all ideas, but only of what I call the 'intellectual concepts', that is to say, of those upon the structure of which arguments concerning objective fact may hinge" (*ibid.*: 272).

Peirce's various writings on pragmatism did not generate any immediate enthusiasm. No doubt intellectual historians will eventually be able to give a more comprehensive account of the reasons for this. But meanwhile, leaving aside Peirce's failure to secure a permanent academic position,[3] three considerations stand out. Peirce's writing style, although not obscure, lacked the clarity and crispness that might have made his views more readily accessible to a wider audience. And, the other two factors exacerbated matters. First, Peirce's philosophical agenda was jam-packed with considerations that were often obliquely connected with pragmatism: anti-Cartesianism; clarification of scientific method; the relationship between belief and doubt; induction; the role of signs in cognition; the nature of logic; and so forth. This must have made it difficult for readers to pick out exactly what it was that made pragmatism different from Peirce's many other enthusiasms. Secondly, there was an air of ambiguity in Peirce's overall attitude towards pragmatism that again must have made it harder for readers to understand what it was supposed to amount to. For Peirce soon objected to the abuses that he regarded the term 'pragmatism' itself as being subjected to "occasionally in literary journals", although his differences with James on this score must have weighed in more heavily. He therefore announced "the birth of the word 'Pragmaticism'", a word "ugly enough to be safe from kidnappers" (*ibid.*: 255). This put his prospective audience in a difficult position, if only because Peirce did not proceed to show in any detail what it was about Pragmaticism that made it sufficiently superior to prevailing interpretations of pragmatism to justify such an off-putting name. Those who were

19

unsure about the nature of pragmatism were made none the wiser by this change of nomenclature.

Enter James

The trail of the human serpent is over everything, as James said, but this does not toss us into the sea of postmodern arbitrariness, where truth varies from person to person and culture to culture.   (Cheryl Misak, *New Pragmatists*)

William James was a lively, engaging and versatile thinker whose writings on both psychology and religion would have ensured his fame had he never entered the field of philosophy.[4] But enter he did, and with no little impact.

James first publicly stated a commitment to pragmatism in the aptly titled lecture "Philosophical Conceptions and Practical Results" delivered at the University of California at Berkeley in 1898. But, indications that his way of thinking was already likely to turn in that direction can be found a good deal earlier. In, for example, his article "The Sentiment of Rationality", we find him claiming, in good pragmatist spirit, that "every way of classifying a thing is but a way of handling it for some purpose" (James 1970: 14).

However, it was with a series of lectures delivered at Wellesley College, the Lowell Institute and Columbia University, in 1905, 1906 and 1907, respectively, that James made the considerable impact just referred to. These lectures were gathered together and published in 1907, "as delivered without development or notes" according to James himself (PMT: 5) under the title *Pragmatism*.[5] The effect *was* considerable, both in the short and longer term. But, it was double edged. James's vivid prose and his ability to connect philosophy imaginatively to a variety of general human concerns conspired to put pragmatism firmly on the intellectual map.[6] Later, it would become clear, as Dewey (2004) predicted, that James had penned a classic, a perennial source of provocative, colourful and insightful ideas that remain fresh and instructive to this day. At the time, it may even have looked to some as if James's somewhat playful hope that pragmatism would spark something momentous, something on the scale of the

Protestant Revolution, had a chance of being fulfilled. However, the 'other edge' soon put paid to that. *Pragmatism* provoked sharp criticism from philosophers who had already made their own impact and had their own philosophical agenda to establish. Chief among these were the British philosophers Russell and Moore.

Pragmatism buzzed with a wealth of ideas that dealt with, for example, differences in philosophical temperament (James introduced his famous distinction between tender and tough-minded thinkers), the nature of theories, the possibility of reconciling philosophy with religion and the pragmatist approach to a number of traditional metaphysical problems. However, Russell and Moore homed in on the account of truth, and in doing so provided the sharp end for a line of criticism contributed to by, among others, George Santayana, Josiah Royce and Arthur O. Lovejoy: Pragmatism elevates "expedient, novel, narrowly instrumental, and technocratic considerations above truth and goodness as revealed by philosophy, art, or theology" (Kloppenberg 1998: 85). In the hands of further cultural commentators, including Lewis Mumford, Van Wyck Brooks and Randolph Bourne, this criticism was also levelled at Dewey.

Indeed, before we consider the stultifying effects that the objections spearheaded by Russell and Moore had on pragmatism, we need to bring Dewey into the picture.

Critical enquiry: Dewey

The most influential pragmatist in the twentieth century has been John Dewey.   (H. O. Mounce, *The Two Pragmatisms*)

Philosophies have too often tried to forego the actual work that is involved in penetrating the true nature of experience, by setting up a purely theoretical security and certainty.

(John Dewey, *Experience and Nature*)

When he began to develop his own conception of pragmatism, under the influence of Peirce and James, Dewey was already highly respected within the fields of both education and psychology. Interestingly, like Peirce, and to a lesser extent James, he had qualms about the very term

21

'pragmatism', although it seems these were fostered by the controversy and misconceptions that came to surround it rather than his perception of any flaw in the meaning of the word itself.

At first blush, Dewey's approach to pragmatism seems to combine the scientific thrust of Peirce's with the humanistic bent of James's, and hence offers the prospect of a pleasing compromise. This impression is certainly borne out in Dewey's aspirations, at least. For throughout his lengthy and productive philosophical career, he sought to preserve for philosophical thinking the kind of rigour that science prides itself on, rigour that would divert it from esoteric disputes, making it more applicable to the practical concerns of real life. On closer inspection, however, it becomes clear that Dewey's position was much nearer to James's and his many references to science involve a broad understanding of its role that is far removed from Peirce's narrower and more conventional one. Dewey gives the game away at the end of chapter 4 of *Experience and Nature*, one of the great works from the very productive last twenty-five years of his life: "The genuine interests of 'pure' science are served only by broadening the idea of application to include all phases of liberation and enrichment of human experience" (EN: 165). Dewey did not want philosophy to be assimilated to science conceived of as a discipline for measuring, predicting and manipulating elements of the material world. He believed that philosophy ought to match science in terms of sensitivity to the things that open-ended enquiry revealed about those elements. And this shows up clearly in Dewey's formulation of "a first-rate test of the value of any philosophy", his counterpart to Peirce's original 'principle' and James's various versions of it:

> Does it end in conclusions which, when they are referred back to ordinary life-experiences and their predicaments, render them more significant, more luminous to us and make our dealing with them more fruitful? Or does it terminate in rendering the things of ordinary experience more opaque than they were before, and in depriving them of having, in 'reality' even the significance they had previously seemed to have? Does it yield the enrichment and increase of power of ordinary things which the results of physical science afford when applied in every-day affairs? (*Ibid.*: 7)

However, Dewey also held that both science and philosophy should subordinate their aims to that of furthering the human good. What Dewey most admired about science, and found lacking in traditional philosophy, was its capacity to innovate in pursuit of this aim: "In scientific inquiry, refined methods justify themselves by opening up new fields of subject-matter for exploration; they create new techniques of observation and experimentation" (*ibid.*: 34). To play catch up in its own endeavours on behalf of the human good, philosophy needed to break the ties to many of its traditional methods, those that rely too heavily, if not exclusively, on first principles, *a priori* assumptions and abstract reasoning. But, it would get nowhere by simply imitating science.

Moreover, as Cornel West (1989: 98) astutely reminds us, an important distinction needs to be marked out to clarify why the scientific tenor of Dewey's rhetoric did not commit him to the *scientistic* conception of philosophy that 'popular opinion' attributed to him. This conception regards scientific method as the sole means of gaining access to fresh and worthwhile knowledge.[7] The fact that Dewey wanted to reshape philosophy under the inspiration of science does not entail that philosophy needs to actually become a form of science or adopt its methods in any fine detail.[8] Those who persist in thinking that Dewey believed it has to do this, on the basis of his frequent references to, and praise of, the achievements of science or simply his propensity to use 'scientific method' as a catchphrase, have failed to distinguish 'scientific attitude' and 'scientific method'.

The scientific attitude, which Dewey endorsed, involves the application of critical intelligence to the practical problems that human beings need to resolve in order to lead better lives. This kind of intelligence involves a willingness to try things out and to revise previously accepted beliefs in the light of the results of such experimentation, while, all the time, keeping in close touch with practical human concerns.[9] By contrast, Dewey regarded scientific method itself as just *one way* of tackling such problems, one that "has no monopoly on what is true and real ... [and] ... provides one kind of description (or set of descriptions) of the world among other kinds of equally acceptable descriptions, e.g., those of art" (West 1989: 98).

Dewey devoted considerable time and energy to explaining how philosophy had hitherto suffered from a tendency to create its own problems in reflective isolation, thereby alienating the public at large and ruining its chances of contributing to social progress. He appealed to the scientific attitude, for purposes of comparison, in getting this point across: "The things of ordinary experience do not get enlargement and enrichment of meaning [in the philosophical approach] as they do when approached through the medium of scientific principles and reasoning" (EN: 6).

Dewey focused on a number of specific examples to illustrate his general line of criticism to the effect that philosophy had been too inclined to detach itself from everyday life by fostering an "arbitrary, aloof, [and] abstract subject-matter, something which exclusively occupies a realm of its own without contact with the things of ordinary experience" (*ibid.*). His treatment of experience is typical in this respect. First, he described how philosophy characterized it. Then he showed how this very characterization generated philosophical problems. And, finally, he introduced ways of talking about experience within which such problems need not arise and, moreover, make little sense if they are invoked.

According to Dewey, philosophy created a notion of experience as something separate from nature, something "too casual and sporadic in its occurrence to carry with it any implications regarding the nature of Nature", and which, in any case, "forms a veil or screen which shuts us off from nature" (*ibid.*: 1a).

The characterization spawned a host of tricky questions that, over time, took on a life of their own as official philosophical problems. They became, for example, problems involving epistemology (e.g. if experience is separate from the world, how can we have any experience-enriched knowledge of the world? How can we know that what we experience has anything to do with what the world is actually like?) and personal identity (e.g. if experience occurs in isolation, how can we explain the existence of minds other than our own? How can we make sense of our own identity as persons embedded in both culture and the material world?).

Dewey held that such problems are parasitic on an overly narrow conception of experience, a conception that derives from philosophy's inclination to conjure up mysteries out of its own dichotomizing theories: "Traditional theories have separated life from nature, mind from organic life, and thereby created mysteries" (*ibid.*: 78).

But rather than demonstrate this in great detail, he moved on to advocate a wider portrayal, one that, in being "inclusive", as he put it, did not feed into the philosophy's traditional problematic. In this portrayal, he again used science as a sounding board: "In the natural sciences there is a union of experience and nature which is not greeted as a monstrosity. The investigator assumes as a matter of course that experience, controlled in specifiable ways, is the avenue that leads to facts and laws of nature" (*ibid.*: 2a). To forestall the objection that this account of scientific practice begs all the interesting and important philosophical issues, Dewey elaborates on various other ways, some commonplace, some not so, in which experience incorporates what it has been philosophically deemed to exclude:

> Experience is no infinitesimally thin layer or foreground of nature ... it penetrates into it, reaching down into its depths, and in such a way that its grasp is capable of expansion; it tunnels in all directions and in doing so brings to the surface things at first hidden ... experience is *of* as well as *in* nature. It is not experience which is experienced but nature – stones, plants, animals, diseases, health, temperature, electricity, and so on. Things interacting in certain ways *are* experience; they are what is experienced. (*Ibid.*: 3a, 4a)

Of course, simply devising ways of talking about the world within which certain philosophical problems do not arise is not sufficient. Unreflective, dogmatic or grossly ignorant people do this effortlessly all the time. The point is to construct an alternative vocabulary that is as flexible and useful for all general purposes as the one it is supposed to replace. Then, since, for all practical purposes, nothing is missing, the absence of particular philosophical mysteries will be of no disadvantage. They will soon be forgotten.

Notice that the criterion 'for all practical purposes' is vital here. It is the linchpin of classic pragmatism. And unfortunately the question as to whether Dewey's account of experience fulfilled that criterion was largely ignored because the criterion itself came under such heavy fire, creating the impression that pragmatism suffered from a fatal weakness and should itself be ignored.

Pragmatism's misunderstanders

We should never have spoken elliptically. The critics have bog-
gled at every word they could boggle at, and refused to take the
spirit rather than the letter of our discourse. This seems to show
a genuine unfamiliarity in the whole view.

(William James, *Pragmatism and The Meaning of Truth*)

The critics of pragmatism have produced only caricatures so
gross as to be unrecognizable and so obscure as to be unintel-
ligible.   (F. C. S. Schiller, *Humanism*)

For the most part, the critics James referred to as "misunderstanders"
(ERP: 265–82) made little effort to gain more familiarity with classic
pragmatism's aims and methods. Tough-minded opponents, epitomized with supercilious wit by Russell ([1908] 1966a, [1909] 1966b)
and somewhat plodding condescension by Moore ([1907] 1960) were
emboldened by the belief that they were in the vanguard of a revolution in philosophy, one that would enable it to at last reach self-
conscious logico-linguistic maturity. Since they believed they had
already discovered the right way to do philosophy, they could not
conceive of there being any value in considering pragmatism on its
own terms. They kicked sand in the face of the very idea of tying
philosophy to any criterion of mere practicality.[10] In doing so, they
obscured classic pragmatism's philosophical potential and blocked
its whole agenda of social improvement. It was, for the time being,
relegated to the sidelines as a relic of intellectual history.

James and Dewey did little to help their own cause. Indeed, they
probably harmed it by spending far too much time engaging with their
critics on the critics' own territory. Thus, for example, instead of enlarg-
ing and developing the wealth of fertile ideas contained in *Pragmatism*,
James devoted most of the sequel, *The Meaning of Truth*, to going back
over old ground to answer his critics on their terms; that is, by taking *their* presuppositions seriously. James seemed to accept that it was
necessary, for instance, to defend a pragmatist account of truth against
the charge that it failed to cater for various intuitions that shore up a
correspondence account of truth: that there is a reality independent of
human concerns, that human claims to knowledge can be deemed true

only when they match up to the appropriate features of that reality, and so on. Dewey was also caught up in much the same way.[11] And although, when he did return to ploughing his own field of thought, he carved out something of a name for himself as a distinguished public intellectual, his body of work exerted little influence on philosophy itself.

Looking back on the manner in which classic pragmatism's critics were so careless in their reading of the relevant texts and so blind to some of James's and Dewey's key insights, it may seem tempting to carry out a counterfactual thought experiment in which the historical record is set straight, the obstacles thrown up by those critics are overcome and pragmatism emerges triumphant. Indeed, some philosophers seem to think that the New Pragmatists, and Rorty in particular, have drawn attention away from the possibility of such an experiment and, in the process, prevented classic pragmatism from rising up again as a potent philosophical force. These thinkers regard the New Pragmatism as an ersatz phenomenon: one that tries to buy philosophical credibility on the cheap by trading on its ancestor's superficially tarnished, but ultimately good, name. All of this is mistaken, and on at least two counts.

First, the classic pragmatism that might emerge victorious from such a re-encounter with its early critics would still be burdened by its heavy debts to the philosophical past. It was not just vociferous critical reactions that held key figures such as James and Dewey back. They were independently wedded to empiricist notions, the most noteworthy being 'experience', that have now been superseded by the "conviction that the problems of philosophy must be addressed through the analysis of language" (Bird 2009: 154), a conviction embraced when philosophy took its famous 'linguistic turn'. Scraping away the excrescences left by an initially hostile reception will not, by itself, be sufficient to revive classic pragmatism.

And secondly, the New Pragmatists are well aware of classic pragmatism's deficiencies in this respect. Far from trading too cheaply on its good name, they have paid tribute to its inspirational features, those that transcend its ties to outmoded philosophical approaches, while, at the same time, taking pains to expose aspects that failed to stand the test of time.

Rorty, for example, frequently endorsed classic pragmatism's abiding concern for the practical (e.g. "Pragmatists think that if something makes no difference in practice, it should make no difference to philosophy"; 1998b: 19), but was nevertheless keen to separate this concern from any formal empiricist underpinning. He thus criticized Dewey for making much too much in general of the notions of 'empirical method' and 'experience', arguing that what Dewey had to say about combating traditional dualisms makes better sense when both are discarded.[12] Both James and Dewey were excited by what they viewed as their radical attempts to push empiricism to the limits. However, Rorty thought pragmatism would be better off drawing sustenance from later thinkers, such as Donald Davidson, who "would rather forget empiricism than radicalise it" (1998b: 292).

In "Dewey Between Darwin and Hegel" (*ibid.*: 290–306), an insightful essay that put Dewey's thought in an illuminating historical context by highlighting the tensions between his Hegelian and Darwinian impulses, Rorty suggested that the elaborate attempts to reformulate a conception of experience that dissolved traditional dualisms, because it was 'inclusive', "more concrete, more holistic" (*ibid.*: 298) and so forth, were not worth the effort involved. He pointed out that both James and Dewey still bought into the framework of ideas that fostered such dualisms. To free themselves, they needed to abandon the very task of squaring experience with reality.[13] But to do that, they would have had to take a significant step forwards in history so that they could then "construe 'thinking' as simply the use of sentences – both for purposes of arranging cooperative enterprises and for attributing inner states (beliefs, desires) to our fellow humans" (*ibid.*). Ironically, such a step, one that involves considering truth as a predicate of sentences rather than experiences, was made within the very tradition that in its formative stages tied pragmatism up in knots of traditional problems thereby ensuring that it would never move in that direction. In the analytic tradition, following the work of Wilfrid Sellars and Davidson in particular, with Ludwig Wittgenstein exerting considerable influence from the side, as it were,[14] experience can be dropped out of the picture when it comes to explaining the relationship between language and the world.[15]

The New Pragmatism

The new pragmatism is just the best of the old pragmatism, undistorted by narcissistic anthropocentrism and developed with contemporary resources.

(David Bakhurst, *Pragmatism and Ethical Particularism*)

The New Pragmatism is unabashedly opportunistic. It looks on classic pragmatism as a source of stimulating ideas, and is especially attracted to those connected with fallibilism and antifoundationalism, as well as those that challenge pernicious dualisms or offer a view of truth that does not depend on a notion of mind and social practice-independent reality. But, it does not want to waste time fighting any of the old battles surrounding the philosophical support for those ideas. Moreover, by apparently taking the tradition that deposed classic pragmatism more seriously than it takes itself, the New Pragmatism uses some of its views on language as a springboard to leap beyond the grasp of age-old philosophical difficulties. By viewing human beings as spinners of words and then considering language to be something that is woven and re-woven to cope with the world and its inhabitants rather than a medium of representation,[16] the New Pragmatism does away with philosophy's perennial intermediaries, those items such as ideas, images, sensations and the like that cause so many of its textbook problems. It turns its back on what it takes to be the moribund problems of the philosophical tradition, problems generated by assumptions that it considers to be both dubious and historically optional. At the same time, it leaves classic pragmatism behind in so far as it is enmeshed in those problems by, for example, its empiricist commitments and its correspondingly deep dependence on experience.

The New Pragmatism is a form of pragmatism because, despite having moved on, it nevertheless continues to be motivated by the original example of classic pragmatism. Furthermore, it is generally guided by the maxim "No difference without a practical consequence in tow". Even though classic pragmatism was unable to strike out far under its own steam, the New Pragmatism regards it as an inspiriting ally in its own attempts to divert philosophy from its preoccupation with a set of themes handed down from Plato and render it more applicable to everyday life, more sensitive to human hopes for a better future. But in what sense is the New Pragmatism 'new'?

It is unique in its historical sophistication. This feature will become clearer in Chapter 3, where we take a closer look at Rorty's approach to philosophy. However, it can be briefly summarized as follows. The New Pragmatism shuns large chunks of the philosophical tradition, but it does so for good reasons and out of an acute historical awareness as to what is viable, and hence salvageable, from that tradition. It criticizes philosophy's attempts to conjure up eternal verities, and to transcend history. At the same time, it recognizes that there are times when it is necessary to lift philosophy out of its own history, out of the ruts it has laid down for itself over time. The classic pragmatists tried to do this, but were thwarted by their critics and also their own lack of self-perception as to how continuous some of their own views were with the tradition they wished to buck.

The New Pragmatists have the courage, conviction and imagination to set out on their own, to ask new questions and explore new themes. They also have the benefit of hindsight. They see quite clearly how classic pragmatism was stifled by critics who had little understanding of its approach. So when their opponents try to lock them into combat, very often by imitating the stifling manoeuvres of their forebears, the New Pragmatists have learned to turn the other philosophical cheek, perhaps by changing the subject or pursuing other interests. Their historical sophistication enables them to understand that significant philosophical changes rarely follow a smooth path carved out in advance by reasoned argument. Hence the abrupt discontinuity between their agenda and that of the tradition they seek to move beyond does not tend to trouble them too much.

By cutting its ties to the past, while at the same time heeding some of its lessons, the New Pragmatism has become cosmopolitan and autonomous. And, these features enable it to be both intellectually innovative and politically flexible. It takes up the task of philosophizing with an open mind, tied down by no prior methodology or pre-set agenda, and answerable to no previous tradition. This means that it is not restricted from crossing boundaries, whether geographical or academic. And, it has already had much success in this respect. There is world-wide interest in the New Pragmatism. Some of Rorty's writings have been translated and are much discussed in many different countries, ranging from Poland to Iran. The New Pragmatism's propensity to infiltrate other disciplines is as much in evidence. We examine some examples of this in our final chapter.

As for autonomy, the New Pragmatism breaks with past philosophical attitudes and beliefs that brought classic pragmatism to a halt. But, its attitude to science illustrates nicely how this works out in other ways too. New Pragmatists are not anti-scientific, but nor are they enthralled by scientific method or even Dewey's more benign notion of a scientific attitude. Under the impetus of Rorty's writings, they adopt a Deweyan 'science-provides-one-kind-of-description-amongst-many' approach, but then draw out the full consequences of this. They see no need for a security blanket of rhetorical gestures in the direction of science. They have no desire to invoke science, as Dewey frequently did, to indicate that philosophy is on the correct path. In this sense, New Pragmatists have overcome a source of the 'craving' so graphically depicted by Wittgenstein:

> Our craving for generality has another main source: our pre-occupation with the method of science. I mean the method of reducing the explanation of natural phenomena to the smallest possible number of primitive natural laws; and, in mathematics, of unifying the treatment of different topics by using a generalisation. Philosophers constantly see the method of science before their eyes, and are irresistibly tempted to ask and answer questions in the way science does. This tendency is the real source of metaphysics, and leads the philosopher into complete darkness. (1969: 18)

Finally, the New Pragmatism enjoys the advantage of being neoteric. This means that it is able to benefit from philosophical progress in ways that classic pragmatism could not.[17] Of course, we do not mean this in the trivial sense that classic pragmatism was unable to discern how philosophy was going to fare in the future. It is rather that the New Pragmatism has not bound itself by the sorts of commitments that were always going to hold classic pragmatism back. Of these, empiricism, with the accent on experience, is the principal factor. New Pragmatists are able discard much philosophical baggage by shifting its focus to language. They see no need to appeal to considerations like 'direct contact with reality' or 'evidence-transcendent standards of objectivity' that keep the old philosophical debates churning over, apparently to little or no social benefit.

Codicil: where does this leave classic pragmatism?

The New Pragmatism leaves classic pragmatism behind. But, where does it leave it? And, what shape is it left in?

Despite the antipathy of its rivals, and a certain lack of historical luck, classic pragmatism laid down a significant cultural footprint. This means that its origins, the lives and works of its founders and its historical fate will continue to be studied in detail, and its interpretation is likely to evolve accordingly. It is too soon to write the final chapter. The success of the New Pragmatism entails the failure of classic pragmatism, but not in every respect. Its classic texts have not been plundered into exhaustion. They remain rich sources of ideas and themes. Indeed, the New Pragmatism itself regards them as such, and continues to return to them as both a sounding board and a springboard. It is not inconceivable that these highly fertile and imaginative works will spawn further interesting philosophical developments independently of, and perhaps in opposition to, the New Pragmatism.[18]

3
RORTY AGAINST THE TRADITION

Reading Rorty is not like reading any other philosopher.
(Christopher Voparil, *Richard Rorty*)

Richard Rorty had such an important influence on the New Pragmatism, and in such a variety of ways, that it is worth examining
his approach in the round. And, this can best be done by looking at
how his pragmatism, the New Pragmatism, evolved out of a long and
complex philosophical journey, one that is often misinterpreted with
unfortunate consequences for the reception of his views. Moreover,
certain aspects of that journey help to explain why Christopher Voparil
is exactly right in saying that reading Rorty is a unique experience.

We treat Rorty somewhat differently from Putnam (see Chapter
4) in that we say far less, in any explicit sense, about his relationship to the New Pragmatism, and even, for the most part, pragmatism in general. Thus, for instance, we include no separate section
on "Rorty and the New Pragmatism". There are good reasons for this.
Rorty's pragmatism is better understood against the background of
the material presented here, so it is better, especially for readers of
an introductory text such as this one, to get that background out
of the way first. When we come to consider the practical upshot of
Rorty's widespread influence, in Chapter 6, then his relationship to
the New Pragmatism should snap into focus, and the background
element presented here should help readers make better sense of his

interventions in disciplines outside philosophy itself. Also, and this should also become clearer from reading this background material, in advocating and exemplifying a New Pragmatist approach to philosophy, Rorty wanted to draw attention to fresh themes, to air new ways of talking and thinking, rather than to glorify the name of that approach. And, his capacity to do this, to get on with the job without constantly announcing "I am a New Pragmatist", was a sign of great confidence in what he was doing.

Opposing assessments

Rorty became a prominent figure within intellectual culture in general, and thus was known as more than just a philosopher. But even as a philosopher he achieved a uniquely high profile. So we can best start by saying something about this aspect of his journey. A sure sign, although not the only one, that a philosopher has become a 'figure' is when their work cannot easily be dealt with without breaking it up into different periods. Moreover, when this becomes true of a philosopher's own lifetime, and there is already some dispute as to the suitability of the demarcations involved, then we can be fairly certain that the philosopher in question is a major figure. By that criterion, Rorty had been a major philosophical figure for quite some time before his death on 8 June 2007.

Since the landmark publication of his book *Contingency, Irony, and Solidarity* in 1989, Rorty's philosophical writings have commonly been divided into three categories:

1. Those that straightforwardly contribute debates within analytic philosophy.
2. Those that question, or purport to undermine, the presuppositions and main concerns of analytic philosophy.
3. Those that expound, explore, and celebrate what is perhaps best called 'postanalytic pragmatism'.

As befits a 'figure', these three categories match up with three successive time periods. Hence (1) corresponds to 'Early Rorty', someone who made solid, but also ingenious, contributions to analytic philosophy; (2) falls in with 'Middle Rorty', a philosopher who issued a robust challenge to philosophy's traditional self-image, but did not cut his own umbilical cord and hence remained attached to that image in various ways; and (3) covers 'Late Rorty', a thinker who espoused 'postanalytic pragmatism' while, for the most part, roaming free of conventional philosophical boundaries, setting his own agenda as he did so.

Controversy surrounds the philosophical value judgements attached to these different 'periods' and, as part of this, the divisions marked out by the latter are themselves disputed. Those who are most hostile to Rorty tend to fall into two camps. These are divided by the opposing assessments they make of his work over the three periods. Members of the first camp, let us call them 'traditionalists', begrudgingly admit that the 'Early Rorty' notched up significant achievements in analytic philosophy. Here they refer to his contributions to the philosophy of mind via his articles on 'eliminative materialism'. His work on 'transcendental arguments' is sometimes also given a favourable mention. In this latter case, Rorty offered some "revisions of and additions to" P. F. Strawson's "new and improved version of the central argument of the *Transcendental Deduction*" – this being where Kant argues that "the possibility of experience somehow involves the possibility of the experience of objects" (Rorty 1970b: 209).

However, having made the benign concession, such critics then claim that 'Middle Rorty' turned his back on his earlier achievements and set himself on a path that would prevent him from doing any work of further philosophical interest. Of the 'Late Rorty', their view is simply that his writings confirm their verdict as to what happened after he lost his early enthusiasm for analytic philosophy: his mature writings are philosophically suspect, and can even be very harmful if taken seriously. For them, there are really only two Rortys. The first is the plain 'analytic Rorty', a thinker they admire and respect and would continue to do so if only he had kept on the straight and narrow. As for the second, the more colourful 'rogue-pragmatist Rorty', they regard him as someone who went off the philosophical rails and most unfortunately made quite a name for himself in doing so.

In the other camp are various philosophers who work outside the analytic tradition, but mainly within the European fold. We can call these the 'continentals'. They are also rather annoyed with Rorty, although on diametrically opposed grounds. For them, Early Rorty was just one more example of an analytic philosopher who helped marginalize, or at best trivialize, a great tradition of serious thinking that runs from Hegel through Nietzsche and onwards down to Heidegger, Foucault and Derrida. It is Middle and Late Rorty that they fiercely object to. Here, they do not accept the traditionalists' view that Rorty betrayed analytic philosophy. It is rather that they feel Rorty betrayed *them*. They are suspicious of the idea that Rorty rebelled against analytic philosophy. They do not accept that he ever broke free of it, and regard his writings on non-analytic thinkers, such as Heidegger and Derrida, as insidious attempts to re-establish the hegemony of the analytic approach. In their eyes, Rorty's brand of pragmatism with extra-analytical trimmings is something of a Trojan horse. Again, there are only two Rortys. Neither is valued, although the reasons for this differ. In the first case it is mainly a matter of indifference, whereas in the second, on the grounds, presumably, that an enemy who poses as your friend is the deadliest enemy of all, there is quite open hostility.

It is against this background of highly contentious disputes that Rorty's philosophical writings must currently be interpreted and assessed. But before we say much more about the significance of such disputes and whether they are likely to ever be resolved, we should fill in some of the details regarding Rorty's personal history and the chronology of his major writings.

Radical beginnings

At 12, I knew that the point of being human was to spend one's life fighting social injustice.

(Richard Rorty, *Philosophy and Social Hope*)

Rorty was born on 4 October 1931 in New York. He was raised within a politicized family that consorted with many of the key progressive thinkers of the day and encouraged leftist activism. No doubt this at least partly explains Rorty's lifelong interest in politics,[1] and perhaps also his ability to engage with social issues in a knowledgeable, clear-minded and accessible manner even though he opted to pursue a purely academic career after studying philosophy at the Universities of Chicago and Yale. That career turned out to be a distinguished one. In 1961, Rorty moved from his first main teaching post at Wellesley College to one of the most prominent and accomplished departments of philosophy in the world at Princeton University, where he taught for over twenty years. He then transferred to the University of Virginia, spending another fifteen extremely productive years there, before taking up his final appointment, still as prolific as ever, in the Department of Comparative Literature at Stanford University. He was an Emeritus Professor of Stanford at the time of his death.

Rorty's first notable writings concerned, as we said above, the philosophy of mind and transcendental arguments. In a series of intricate and influential articles (e.g. Rorty 1965, 1970a), he took up the cause of 'materialism', advocating an 'eliminative' or 'disappearance' account of the relationship between sensations and brain processes. On this account, the language associated with the former, language that is supposed to designate or describe subjective experiences, is fated to 'disappear' or be 'eliminated' from discourse. It might linger on for some purposes of social interaction, but it will play no role in a proper philosophical explanation of the nature of the mind. To the obvious retort that it is absurd to imply, as his own account seems to, that words like 'itch', 'burn' and 'pain' will be made redundant when they are replaced by other words that have a purely physical reference point, Rorty responded with the kind of insouciance about the possibility of a radical change in linguistic usage under the pressure of social convenience that his critics would later find provocative:

> [the] absurdity of saying 'Nobody has ever felt a pain' is no greater than that of saying 'Nobody has ever seen a demon' *if* we have a suitable answer to the question 'What was I reporting when I said I felt a pain?' To this question, the science of the future may reply, "You were reporting the occurrence of a certain brain-process and it would make life simpler for us if you would in future *say* 'My C-fibres are firing' instead of saying 'I'm in pain'". (1965: 30)

Rorty also published a number of articles on the general theme of 'Transcendental Arguments', taking his cue, as we indicated earlier, from Strawson's attempt to reconstruct an improved version of Kant's anti-sceptical strategy. The major claim that Rorty was seeking to establish has been well summarized by Anthony Brueckner: "If one is a self-conscious being and therefore possesses the concept of an experience, then one also possesses the concept of a physical object" ([1983] 2002: 173). If Rorty had published nothing other than the work we have referred to so far, he would still have warranted an honorary footnote in any adequate account of the analytic chapter in philosophy's history. Indeed, this may be understating the case. For, his early work is now attracting renewed interest. It is likely to be more positively assessed as a result of this, not least because, as Robert Brandom points out, Rorty's contributions displayed considerable originality that went largely unnoticed:

[He was] the author of the first genuinely new response to the traditional mind–body problem that anyone had seen in a long time [and] came to a new way of thinking about one of Descartes' central innovations: his definition of the mind in *epistemic* terms. (Brandom 2000b: 157)[2]

Charles Guignon and David Hiley reinforce Brandom's upbeat reassessment when they claim that

in retrospect, we can see that Rorty's eliminative materialism, then claimed to be merely one among various alternative positions available in the debate over mind–body identity, was actually an attempt to undermine the entire modern (Cartesian) tradition that organised the world in terms of mind and matter. (2002: 6)

However, it was the next stage in Rorty's publishing career that catapulted him into a higher league and set the stage for his appearance as a far more provocative and influential thinker, and the architect of the New Pragmatism.

Challenging the tradition

The picture which holds traditional philosophy captive is that of
the mind as a great mirror, containing various representations
– some accurate, some not – and capable of being studied by
non-empirical means.

(Richard Rorty, *Philosophy and the Mirror of Nature*)

The work that apparently marked out this next stage was *Philosophy
and the Mirror of Nature*, a book that soon gained sufficient notoriety to match the scale of its ambition.[3] *Philosophy and the Mirror
of Nature* was ambitious in the sense that it sought to free modern Western philosophy from its perennial problems, the kinds of
problems that had concerned it, in one way or another, since the
Greeks. And what seemed so disreputable to Rorty's opponents was
the *way* in which *Philosophy and the Mirror of Nature* attempted to
achieve this goal. For it did not seek to solve these problems or even
offer detailed arguments to show that they were not really serious
problems at all. Instead, it wove a complex quasi-historical narrative within which the problems in question appeared to be entirely
optional. Furthermore, it claimed to have detected an 'internal dialectic' by means of which some of the key players in modern analytic
philosophy marked out the first important steps towards the conclusion of this narrative.

In taking this approach Rorty appeared to be doing philosophy
itself a great disservice. He implied that its traditional subject matter could be sidestepped with impunity, that it was no longer worth
taking time out to try to answer the sorts of questions the greatest
philosophers had battled with down the ages. Many of Rorty's critics
carried this further, regarding *Philosophy and the Mirror of Nature* as
a concerted attempt to kill off philosophy once and for all. Moreover,
they deeply resented Rorty's insinuation that when philosophy finally
succumbed to his attacks, the hands of a number of important thinkers within the analytic tradition, including Wittgenstein, Sellars, Quine
and Davidson, would perhaps be more bloodstained than his own.[4]
For Rorty claimed that such thinkers had started a process of undermining analytic philosophy that he was merely carrying to its natural
conclusion. Much ink was wasted in combating his supposed role as

the would-be undertaker. This was a mistake, one that was encouraged by some of the rhetoric in the book, but a mistake nonetheless. As we shall see, Rorty's position on this can be captured by the following line of argument: (1) philosophy has no 'core' subject matter or methodology; (2) *a fortiori* it has no intellectual quintessence; and (3) therefore there is no point in trying to destroy it by intellectual means.

Philosophy and the Mirror of Nature opens with the statement "Almost as soon as I began to study philosophy, I was impressed by the way in which philosophical problems appeared, disappeared, or changed shape as a result of new assumptions or vocabularies" (PMN: xiii). This is important. It paves the way for the fresh conception of the nature of philosophical problems that Rorty developed throughout the book as a whole. It also underpins many of his contributions to the New Pragmatism. Under this conception, philosophy is 'historical' through and through. It has no essential nature that keeps it apart from social events. This means that philosophy does not depend on any *particular* issues, methods or general subject matter. Philosophical problems can *seem* inescapable. But, that is because the background assumptions that generate them, and the vocabularies in which they are described, have already been uncritically accepted. Dig those up for inspection, show how they are rooted in sociohistorical circumstances, and the problems in question may no longer appear compelling. Rorty devoted a considerable portion of *Philosophy and the Mirror of Nature* to showing how philosophical issues concerning the nature of mind and the definition of knowledge arise out of such circumstances.

Rorty believed that these two sets of issues are vital to philosophy's self-image as the 'master discipline'. And, he rightly claimed they are intimately connected. They are vital because once philosophy hijacks them and provides its own account of them, dominion over the rest of culture looks like the next natural step. If philosophers have special knowledge of mind or, more precisely, of what it is that makes minds special, namely consciousness, then they stand in a privileged position with regard to understanding the nature of human beings. Furthermore, when philosophers possess a unique understanding of knowledge, they are in a position to stand in judgement over all other disciplines. These can be ranked according to whether or not they are able to yield genuine knowledge. Philosophy stands at the top of the tree of intellectual culture because only it is qualified to carry out the ranking, only it has the appropriate knowledge required to do this: knowledge of knowledge.

The linkage that we referred to is important because it is only on the general conception of mind that supposedly gives philosophers privileged access to its nature that issues relating to knowledge gain their importance. If consciousness is the differentiating feature of the mind, and it is regarded as a private feature in the sense that its contents can be properly known only from the inside,[5] as it were, then a gap opens up between the mind's 'self-knowledge' and its 'other-knowledge', its knowledge of all other things. Into this gap between mind and the world springs the discipline called 'epistemology', the (philosophical) theory of knowledge. Of course, all this is very schematic, but in *Philosophy and the Mirror of Nature* Rorty painted in enough historical detail to show how the age-old philosophical questions about mind and knowledge – 'How are the mind and body related?', 'How can scepticism about the very possibility of knowledge be overcome?', and so on – become 'philosophical problems' only on the back of a wealth of historically contingent assumptions.

At times, Rorty wrote as if the sheer fact of their 'contingency' is enough to render traditional philosophical problems redundant. This is wrong. From the fact that something is optional it does not follow that this thing is uninteresting, unimportant or best avoided. If we mistakenly believe that chess is a game that we just *have to play* once we discover its existence, its status might well go down in our estimation when we discover that we are wrong about this, wrong to have ever believed that chess-playing is mandatory, but we need not then automatically regard it as trivial, a game we would do rather well to dispose of.

Nevertheless, there is something to what Rorty said. It countered the great myth that the questions philosophers have always tended to concern themselves with are questions that *must* arise as soon as we begin to reflect properly on the world and our relationship with it. And Rorty was right to suggest that here the notion of 'reflecting properly' begs all the interesting questions: that philosophers have failed to show that *other* ways of thinking about the same thing, ways that do not throw up certain kinds of questions, are illegitimate. Furthermore, he had another, more practical, string to his bow.

Put the thought that certain philosophical problems are 'contingent', in the sense we have just alluded to, together with the thought that the practical benefits of tackling these problems over the years have been meagre at best, and then it seems perfectly reasonable to suggest that they be set aside. This was Rorty's own proposal in *Philosophy and the Mirror of Nature*. It is not that we should sideline such problems simply because *we can*; it is rather that, having seen they are no longer compelling (the 'contingency' claim) and having noted that nothing much has been gained from treating them as if they *are* compelling (the 'lack of practical results' claim), moving on from them would be a very sensible thing for our culture to do. However, Rorty's account of what moving on involves also provoked controversy. Rorty himself was to blame for this. But, his critics are also partly culpable for not reading him carefully enough.

Rorty was at fault because of an unfortunate structural ambiguity that he allowed to infect the composition of *Philosophy and the Mirror of Nature*. The book weaves a complex, meandering narrative, but it always appears to be moving in one climactic direction: to a place where, after abandoning their fruitless, traditional pursuits, philosophers are finally concerned with what they ought to be concerned with. In this place, or so readers might be deceived into thinking, philosophers spend all their time practising what, towards the end of *Philosophy and the Mirror of Nature*, Rorty flagged as 'hermeneutics'. But, if readers are so deceived, and clearly many have been, they will be puzzled as to what the term 'hermeneutics' means. They will be thwarted if they think that, having reached the final section of the book, which is simply entitled "Philosophy", they will discover what philosophy should be all about if only they crack the meaning of 'hermeneutics'. Earlier, in chapter four, the chapter he regarded as central to the book, Rorty introduced another alternative to traditional epistemology. He called this 'epistemological behaviourism', and glossed it as "explaining rationality and epistemic authority by reference to what society lets us say, rather than the latter by the former" (PMN: 174). However, he never developed this far enough to obviate the thought that 'hermeneutics' was the goal of his narrative account, and that it has plenty of work to do if it is to enable philosophy to survive in any recognizably stable form.

To his credit, and to the detriment of those who allow themselves to be too easily deceived in the way we have just indicated, Rorty made a concerted effort to undermine any expectation that the final section of *Philosophy and the Mirror of Nature* will offer a straightforward alternative to traditional philosophy. With regard to 'hermeneutics', he was quite explicit: "I want to make clear at the outset that I am *not* putting hermeneutics forward as a 'successor subject' to epistemology, as an activity which fills the cultural vacancy once filled by epistemologically centred philosophy" (*ibid.*: 315). However, such efforts were insufficient. And, there are two main reasons why.

First, Rorty should not have expected to get away with creating a structural momentum that seems to be leading to a particular sort of denouement and then, when the time comes, simply announcing that what looks and sounds like 'the final act', in which the key questions raised by the lengthy and meandering plot are at last resolved, is not a final act at all. This was a particularly bad move on Rorty's part given that he had already described the miasmic effect that traditional philosophy has on its practitioners, who must surely have been his target audience. The mistake was compounded, and this is our second reason, by the somewhat elusive way in which Rorty *did* explain the nature of hermeneutics. It was not

> the name for a discipline, nor for a method of achieving the sort of results which epistemology failed to achieve, nor for a program of research. On the contrary, hermeneutics is an expression of hope that the cultural space left by the demise of epistemology will not be filled – that our culture should become one in which the demand for constraint and confrontation is no longer felt. The notion that there is a permanent neutral framework whose 'structure' philosophy can display is that notion that the objects to be confronted by the mind, or the rules which constrain inquiry are common to all discourse, or at least to every discourse on a given topic. Hermeneutics is largely a struggle against this assumption. (*Ibid.*: 315–16)

In addition to 'epistemologial behaviourism' and 'hermeneutics', Rorty invoked three philosophical heroes who are supposed to demonstrate how philosophy can be done outside the tradition that he criticized in *Philosophy and the Mirror of Nature*. These are Dewey, Heidegger and Wittgenstein. At first blush they seem a very mixed, and historically incompatible, bunch. But Rorty displayed remarkable powers of appropriation in managing to find something in the writings of each of them that chimes with what he was trying to do in *Philosophy and the Mirror of Nature*. Thus Dewey was praised for his "conception of knowledge as what we are justified in believing", as someone who enables us to "see 'justification' as a social phenomenon rather than a transaction between 'the knowing subject' and 'reality'" (*ibid.*: 9). And this take on knowledge played an important role in all of Rorty's pragmatist thinking. Heidegger was co-opted as a thinker who found a way of retelling the history of philosophy that "lets us see the beginnings of Cartesian imagery in the Greeks and the metamorphoses of this imagery during the last three centuries". Rorty viewed him as someone who "thus lets us 'distance' ourselves from the tradition" (*ibid.*: 12). And finally, Wittgenstein was called upon on account of his "flair for deconstructing captivating pictures" (*ibid.*). Rorty read Wittgenstein's *Philosophical Investigations* as an attempt to break the spell cast by all previous ambitions, most notably Wittgenstein's own in his *Tractatus*, to turn philosophy into a 'master discipline'. Although his discussion of these 'heroes' touched on some intriguing possibilities for the future development of philosophy, their actual role is not much more than emblematic. Far more needs to be said to head off the kind of concern raised so trenchantly by Bernard Williams:

> I doubt, in fact, whether Rorty has extracted from the ruins, as he sees it, of Philosophy any activity that will sustain a post-Philosophical culture of the kind that he sketches. It is not very realistic to suppose that we could for long sustain much of a culture, or indeed keep away boredom, by playfully abusing the texts of writers who believed in an activity which we now know to be helpless. (1990: 33)

Although Rorty's attempt to describe the transition from traditional philosophy to 'philosophy as endorsed by the tenets of *Philosophy and the Mirror of Nature*' was unsatisfactory, this is not a flaw that lingered to stain the whole of his career. For he later found that the perfect way to solve this problem was by turning *completely* New Pragmatist; that is, by simply philosophizing in a new mode without looking back over his shoulder to see how the tradition was reacting. And he did this with some aplomb in his next major publication, *Contingency, Irony, and Solidarity*, perhaps the first major New Pragmatist text. But, before we look at how he unleashed his imagination in that book, it is worth looking back on the controversial conversational theme at the heart of *Philosophy and the Mirror of Nature*.

Like many great writers, Rorty knew how to capture our attention in short, sharp phrases or sentences that encapsulated the essentials of what he wanted to get across. And, his most memorable aphorisms were self-consciously elliptical. They sparkled against the backcloth of a more considered treatment of the matter in hand couched in what Jonathan Ree aptly called "carefully contrived, plain-dealing prose" (1998: 7). Hence, when Rorty nonchalantly quipped that "Kant simply provides sugar coating for the bitter Platonic pill" (Brandom 2000: 123), it comes as no surprise that there was a characteristically informative gloss on this, one that invoked "two of Kant's earliest readers", Fichte and Hegel (*ibid.*). In this sense, Rorty was more like James than full-blooded aphorists such as Nietzsche.

The comparisons are instructive in that Rorty was, and still is, often treated like a latter-day Nietzsche, as if the *only* words he ever voiced were inflammatory ones. And, come to think of it, James was also treated in the same way by his early critics. He penned bundles of qualifications to stiffen his account of truth against the charge of unbridled subjectivism, as we discussed earlier. These were prescient adjustments that later came to resonate with the holistic themes in the less maligned writings of Quine and Davidson. But, they were shrugged off at the time, and those early critics still made sure that James became known as a philosopher who claimed such mighty strange things as 'A truth is anything it pays to believe' or 'The statement "*X* exists" may be true even if *X* does not exist'. It was only when Rorty struck out on his own regardless of the damage inflicted on pragmatism in its youth, and began to show that some of its ideas could make useful contributions to intellectual culture, that more careful readings of James (e.g. Putnam & Putnam 1995a,b) began to supplant those of the rumour mongers.

Given that Rorty did so much to help restore James's reputation as a philosopher to be reckoned with, it is ironic that his own writings have been abused by critics who, by skimming off quotations and refusing to see any light beyond their own entrenched assumptions, threaten to make history repeat itself. Nowhere is the folly of their excesses more apparent than in their vitriolic responses to Rorty's pregnant suggestion in *Philosophy and the Mirror of Nature* that conversation should replace confrontation as the main determiner of intellectual beliefs. The conversation Rorty has in mind involves, but does not *only* involve, the kind of refined communicative exchanges that produce cultural goods such as novels, poems and even scientific theories. And, the confrontation he wishes us to forswear is the alleged correspondence between the content of the claims we hold to be true and the world those claims are held to be true of. Some of Rorty's critics react to this as if he is shamelessly urging us to gorge on the fruits of inane chatter, thereby exposing ourselves to the risk of losing all regard for more noble attempts to formulate world-constrained beliefs. In short, they take conversational limits on beliefs to mean 'coffee-shop limits'. And, this sounds to the traditional philosophical ear awfully like no limits at all. But, when we turn to *Contingency, Irony, and Solidarity*, we find that Rorty refused to be held back by such insensitivity: that in switching to a conversational mode he found some very interesting things to say indeed.

Liberal ironists

In *Philosophy and the Mirror of Nature*, Rorty tried to show that "the notion of knowledge as the assemblage of accurate representations is optional" (PMN: 11). He then went on to generalize this endeavour, by trying to also show that even the most recent advances in philosophy, for example in the philosophy of language and the philosophy of mind, have failed to escape the hypnotic effects of this 'notion': that the philosophers concerned are still labouring under the illusion that they can construct a "permanent, neutral framework of inquiry, and thus for all culture" (*ibid.*: 8). We pointed out that to show a philosophical problem to be 'historically optional' is not, *by itself*, sufficient to show that it should be abandoned. In *Contingency, Irony, and Solidarity*, Rorty painted a much broader picture of 'contingency'. And, in this picture, philosophy loses its veneer of necessity, of dealing with issues we *must* confront, not just because the claims it makes and the methods it uses to support these claims are optional, but also because the very world in which philosophy has to find roots, and in some sense account for, is rife with 'contingencies'. Rorty's overall aim was to show us how to become friends with the idea, so inimical to the analytic tradition, that everything in our lives is the 'product of time and chance'.

He deployed three main strategies in *Contingency, Irony, and Solidarity* to foster and then enliven this kind of 'friendship', one that he felt, for the reason just alluded to, would be especially difficult for many philosophers. First, in the opening three chapters, he redescribed large areas of our lives in ways that revealed the ubiquity of 'time and chance'. These areas involved our use of language, our sense of personal identity and our conception of community. Rorty's second strategy was to show how relatively recent developments in our intellectual culture have prepared us for such a redescription. Whether or not we know it, the time is ripe for us to come to terms with the part that chance plays in human affairs. Finally, Rorty provided a handy vocabulary that we can use to talk to each other in terms that do not involve, and indeed celebrate our liberation from, ahistorical myths.

In working through these strategies, Rorty did something quite unusual, perhaps unique. He introduced a series of important themes, such as the nature of human identity, that resonated with traditional philosophical concerns, and he did this in a way that makes it clear that *Contingency, Irony, and Solidarity* definitely belongs in the 'philosophy' section of libraries; so, for example, the names of many philosophers were mentioned. However, in doing this, the book ushered readers into new territory, beyond the borders marked out by traditional philosophical writings. Moreover, Rorty spent very little time constructing arguments for particular theses, and when he tackled a theme that seemed to emerge out of the long tradition stretching at least as far back as Plato, he put a special spin on it that lifted it above the kind of philosophical concerns that were the lifeblood of that tradition. He did this mainly by undercutting the dominant images and metaphors behind these concerns and then replacing them with new ones: ones that arose out of a more 'literary' approach to philosophy. In *Philosophy and the Mirror of Nature,* Rorty tried to show that attempts to make language answerable to reality itself were bound to end in philosophical tears. This put different uses of language, for example scientific as opposed to fictional, on the same footing. It thus cleared the path for poets and novelists to make a more significant contribution to philosophy. For they are able to bend language into shapes that make life richer and more interesting and thus achieve philosophical goals that, for Rorty, made more sense than the traditional one of fidelity to the facts, or, more simply, 'truth'.

Take the case of personal identity. Philosophical debates on this topic have been generated by a basic, 'essentialist' assumption: there must be something that distinguishes a human being from other entities; there must be something that makes me who I am.[6] This assumption is culturally embedded, and many philosophers from Hume to Parfit have tried to refute it. The candidates for the special 'something' here range from 'the soul' to 'reason', 'consciousness' or even 'social convention'. Rorty did not attempt to enter the debate as to whether such candidates are either necessary or suitable. Instead, he jumped straight into a roving discussion of fresh issues concerning our sense of 'selfhood'. In this discussion previous philosophical considerations fall naturally by the wayside. And, as these fresh issues grab our attention, it no longer seems important to answer the old questions about personal identity, questions such as: does the self have a non-contingent core, and if it does what criteria can we use to identify it?

Rorty kicked off the discussion independently of the thinkers whose work raises these 'old questions', thinkers such as Descartes and Locke. Instead, he started with some reflections on the final sections of Philip Larkin's poem "Continuing to Live". He took the main theme of the poem to be the fear of dying, where the poet's main aim is to make the nature of this 'fear' more explicit by reflecting on what it is that has to die, "what it is that will not be" (CIS: 23). These reflections suggested to Rorty that there were ways of pursuing and then developing Larkin's line of interest that avoid traditional philosophical worries about the self being extinguished, worries such as whether, when death looms, some special, soul-like substance or entity, some 'essence' of the person involved, is about to be preserved or erased. Apprehension about 'what it is that will not be' need not be met with Socratic ploys, designed to tease out, or show the impossibility of, a final definition of 'the self'.

What Larkin feared most, according to Rorty, was the dissipation of "his idiosyncratic lading-list, his individual sense of what was possible and important. That is what made him different from all the other I's" (*ibid.*: 23). Larkin's apprehension concerns what was unique in his body of work, what was special about the various poems he has created. The outcome he dreaded was that his poetic creations would merely be seamlessly absorbed into the anonymity of mass culture: that, in the end, "nobody will find anything distinctive in them" (CIS: 24). The moral Rorty drew here is that creative people may well worry that

> The words (or shapes, or theorems, or models of physical nature) marshalled to one's command may seem merely stock items, rearranged in routine ways … [in which case] One will not have impressed one's mark on language but rather, will have spent one's life shoving about already coined pieces. (*Ibid.*)

Such comments may seem to have been leading us away from traditional philosophical issues, deep issues regarding 'death' and 'the self', and at the cost of having to entertain some rather mundane thoughts about 'originality' in art and other forms of creativity. However, Rorty's next sentence cut straight through such an impression: "So one would not really have had an I at all" (*ibid.*). For this contention shifts the whole discussion even further away from essentialist queries as to what constitutes 'selfhood' to a more open-ended discussion concerning the possibilities of *creating* a self.

In this discussion, worries about what is already 'given' in the constitution of the self are no longer relevant. What matters is what has been 'made'. But, we should not take it that Rorty was arguing for any thesis along the lines of 'The self is nothing until it is created'. He was not saying that the traditional approach is wrong because it failed to subscribe to such a thesis, but rather something like this: 'Here is a potentially interesting way of talking about the self, one that does require the continuation of sterile traditional debates. Let's try it out!'

49

Having broken free from traditional philosophical worries about personal identity, Rorty branched out to anticipate the objection that his way of 'talking about the self' was too specialized: that, although it might be fine for leading artistic figures, it ignored the ordinary person, the person not just lacking, but incapable of producing, creative output. Rorty countered the claim that his approach to 'selfhood' catered only for history's chosen ones, the creative elite, by appealing to Nietzsche and Freud and, in the process, moved even further beyond the preoccupations of traditional philosophers. Nietzsche was piped on board because he identified "the strong poet, the maker, as humanity's hero", urged us to become "the poets of our own lives" (see Rorty 2007: 110), and regarded "self knowledge as self creation" (CIS: 27). But it was only when Freud was invoked that it became clear how Rorty's approach could be generalized to include just about everyone. In Rorty's view, Freud democratized Nietzsche by making it plausible to believe that the minutiae of *each life* is the stuff of poetry, the raw material for self-knowledge – a point anticipated in more lofty terms by Keats in *The Fall of Hyperion: A Dream*:

Who alive can say,
"Though art no Poet – mayst not tell thy dreams"?
Since every man whose soul is not a clod
Hath visions, and would speak, if he had loved,
And been well nurtured in his mother tongue.
                    (*The Fall of Hyperion*, in Keats 1988: 435)

Rorty's Freud put a mundane spin on this. All of us generate 'creative output' simply by living:

Freud's account of unconscious fantasy shows us how to see every human life as a poem – or more exactly, every human life not so racked by pain as to be unable to learn a language nor so immersed in toil as to have no leisure in which to generate a self-description. He sees every life as an attempt to clothe itself in metaphors.   (CIS: 35–6)

Rorty developed this discussion further by making it clear that Freud should not be construed as someone who makes assertions in

"the traditional philosophical reductionist way", but rather as someone who "just wants to give us one more redescription of things to
be filed alongside all the others, one more vocabulary, one more set
of metaphors which he thinks will have a chance of being used and
thereby literalized" (*ibid.*: 39).

To help make us comfortable with the notion that it is better for
artists and intellectuals to throw creative linguistic possibilities at us
rather than claims to authoritative knowledge of reality, Rorty invited
us to become 'liberal ironists'. And, he prefaced this invitation with
an outline of what he called a 'final vocabulary':

> All human beings carry about a set of words which they employ
> to justify their actions, their beliefs, and their lives. These are
> the words in which we formulate praise of our friends and con-
> tempt for our enemies, our long-term projects, our deepest self-
> doubts and our highest hopes. They are the words in which we
> tell, sometimes prospectively and sometimes retrospectively,
> the story of our lives. I shall call these words a person's 'final
> vocabulary'. (*Ibid.*: 141)

The philosophical tradition that Rorty wanted us to escape from
has its own vision as to what such a vocabulary should contain. It
should contain those words that capture the nature of reality, words
that can be used to settle, once and for all, any doubts about our relationship to that 'reality'. Naturally, Rorty had a different view. For him,
a final vocabulary was 'final' only in the sense that it was the vocabulary of last *practical resort*: final in the sense that "if doubt is cast upon
the worth of these words, their user has no noncircular argumentative
recourse" (*ibid.*). A 'liberal ironist' is someone who understands the
contingent status of their own final vocabulary and has come to terms
with it. In doing so, although Rorty did not spell this out, they have
tamed 'postmodernism'. For such a person lives comfortably in a state
of what, for a traditional philosopher, looks like radical instability:

1. She has radical and continuing doubts about the final vocabulary she currently uses, because she has been impressed
   by other vocabularies taken as final by people or books she
   has encountered.

51

2. She realizes that argument phrased in her present vocabulary can neither underwrite nor dissolve these doubts.
3. Insofar as she philosophizes about her situation, she does
   not think her vocabulary is closer to reality than others,
   that it is in touch with a power not herself.   (*Ibid.*: 73)

Notice that in the liberal ironist's final vocabulary, philosophical
words have no special standing. They are not banished from such
a vocabulary. Some people will still find nothing better to wrap 'the
story of their lives' in at the time than phrases such as 'categorical
imperatives', 'necessary truths' and 'causal conditionals'. However, if
they are 'ironists' they will have realized that such language has no
inherent advantage over other kinds of words: that it has to compete
with such words on equal terms, having only its practical usefulness
and metaphoric attractiveness to commend it. Rather than trying to
dig down to philosophical bedrock, Rorty encouraged us to reach
out sideways, so to speak, to the work of other creative people in the
culture around us who have forged innovative ways of living with
contingency –people such as Proust:

> Proust temporalized and finitized the authority figures he had
> met by seeing them as creatures of contingent circumstances.
> Like Nietzsche, he rid himself of the fear that there was an
> antecedent truth about himself, a real essence which others
> might have detected. But, Proust was able to do so without
> claiming to know a truth which was hidden from the author-
> ity figures of his earlier years. He managed to debunk author-
> ity without setting himself up as an authority, to debunk the
> ambitions of the powerful without sharing them. He finitized
> authority figures not by detecting what they 'really' were but
> by watching them become different than they had been, and
> by seeing how they looked when redescribed in terms offered
> by still other authority figures, whom he played off against
> the first. The result of all this finitization was to make Proust
> unashamed of his own finitude. He mastered contingency by
> recognizing it, and thus freed himself from the fear that the
> contingencies he had encountered were more than just contin-
> gencies. He turned other people from his judges into his fellow

sufferers, and thus succeeded in creating the taste by which he judged himself. (*Ibid.*: 103)

Contingency, Irony, and Solidarity provided a wealth of other material for creatively bolstering the liberal ironist's confidence without having recourse to standard philosophical forms of justification. The book also tried to show why 'liberalism' and 'irony' are made for one another. For this form of politics provides the individual with the personal space, the freedom, to develop their own vocabularies of self-creation, and is itself ideally served by such a vocabulary because it requires no philosophical underpinning.

In this Late phase of his writings, Rorty gained the confidence to answer the big question left hanging at the end of *Philosophy and the Mirror of Nature*: how can philosophy continue if it breaks away from its ancestral roots and gives up on its traditional ambitions? He did so in true New Pragmatist spirit by simply exploring a number of themes, including personal identity, human solidarity, the nature of cruelty and the public–private distinction, without stopping to find out whether what he was doing was philosophically respectable. The criterion of success for this kind of venture is whether these themes, and Rorty's way of dealing with them, catch on: whether they stimulate enough interest to supplant the abiding concerns of the tradition derided in *Philosophy and the Mirror of Nature*.

Essays against the tradition

We can now see the shape of Rorty's career in broad outline, and we can see how it matches up with the 'Early', 'Middle' and 'Late' characterizations of Rorty mentioned earlier. But to end the story there would be to miss out a vital element: the part that *essays* play in Rorty's philosophical development. These are important not because of the sheer quantity involved (many of them are now collected in four separate volumes; see Rorty 1991a,b, 1998b, 2007), but rather on account of their strategic role. When his essays are taken into consideration, the career shape that we just referred to undergoes a significant deformation, to the extent that the very notion of 'the three

Rortys' is subverted. And this also has a bearing on the controversies we referred to at the start.

This 'subversion' starts very early on: well before *Philosophy and the Mirror of Nature* was published. And it starts not with a volume of Rorty's own essays, but with his substantial thirty-nine-page editorial introduction to a collection of the writings of other philosophers that he gathered together under the title *The Linguistic Turn* (1967). For those who wish to understand Rorty's philosophical development in the round, this 'introduction' is now an important text in its own right, and all the more so since Rorty himself seems to have overlooked its significance. In "Twenty-five Years After", a retrospective essay appended to a later reprinting of *The Linguistic Turn* (1992), Rorty was too busy taking himself to task for a few sentences that celebrated the triumph of 'linguistic philosophy' to notice the disruptive framework he had constructed around those remarks. He said that these remarks now struck him

> as merely the attempt of a thirty-three-year-old philosopher to convince himself that he had the luck to be born at the right time – to persuade himself that the disciplinary matrix in which he happened to find himself (philosophy as taught in most English-speaking unversities in the 60s) was more than just one more philosophical school, one more tempest in an academic teapot.　　　　　　　　　　　　　　　　　　(*Ibid.*: 371)

However, this self-assessment needs to be set against the backcloth of many of Rorty's other introductory remarks, where he demonstrated that he had done some hard thinking about the potential weaknesses of the 'linguistic' approach to philosophy. In these, he displayed an acute sensitivity to the historical context of 'philosophical problems', a lack of enthusiasm for the notion of a universal 'philosophical method', an empathy with classic American pragmatism and a keen interest in meta-philosophical issues, all of which showed him to be out of step with established conceptions of linguistic philosophy. Indeed, he started off by doing something no exponent of this approach would normally be inclined to do: he provided a *historicist*, almost Hegelian, picture of how revolutions in philosophy take place. In this picture he identified a general problem that makes it difficult for any philosopher to rest content that the method of doing philosophy that they have adopted is the right one:

> To know what method to adopt, one must already have arrived at some metaphysical and some epistemological conclusions. If one attempts to defend these conclusions by the use of one's chosen method, one is open to the charge of circularity. If one does not so defend them, maintaining that given these conclusions, the need to adopt the chosen method follows, one is open to the charge that the chosen method is inadequate, for it cannot be used to establish the crucial metaphysical and epistemological theses which are in dispute. Since philosophical method is in itself a philosophical topic (or, in other words, since different criteria for the satisfactory solution of a philosophical problem are adopted, and argued for, by different schools of philosophers), every philosophical revolutionary is open to the charge of circularity or to the charge of having begged the question. *(Ibid.*: 1–2)

It may well be the case that Rorty's early awareness of this 'general problem' was one of the factors that throughout his career, and to the great annoyance of some of his critics, made him so reluctant to 'justify' his own philosophical predilections.[7]

Finally, when reflecting in some detail on how the future of philosophy might unfold, although Rorty was not ungenerous towards linguistic philosophy, the options he described have some striking affinities with his own later writings. These include: (a) linguistic philosophy is regarded "as having led to a dead end"; (b) philosophy "grows closer to poetry"; (c) philosophy is seen "as a cultural disease which has been cured"; and, most presciently, (d) philosophers concern themselves with "the creation of new and fruitful ways of thinking about things in general" (1992: 34–6). The latter option chimes perfectly with the 'redescriptive' rhetoric of *Contingency, Irony, and Solidarity*.

The conclusion to draw here is that the Rorty who gained wider attention on account of the controversy surrounding the publication of *Philosophy and the Mirror of Nature* over a decade later was not some newborn rebel, someone who had only just defected from the analytic camp, but rather a much deeper thinker who, in that book, at last found a way of giving systematic voice to the kinds of concerns and doubts he had since he became a professional philosopher. When the considerable number of Rorty's 'early essays' are made more accessible,[8] more evidence will emerge, even from the heartland of his 'analytic work', to support this assessment.

There is a second manner in which Rorty's essays tend to be 'strategic', and in this case, too, the tripartite characterization of his publishing career comes under pressure. Consider, for example, the thought that *Philosophy and the Mirror of Nature* represents a dramatic turning point in Rorty's career. We have already adduced some evidence against this, but when we turn to essays that he wrote before and just after it, the bulk of which are collected together in *Consequences of Pragmatism* (1982), we find that they also undermine the notion that *Philosophy and the Mirror of Nature* was somehow treasonous: that it showed Rorty to be a turncoat. These essays flesh out some of the material in *Philosophy and the Mirror of Nature*, and to some extent prepare the ground for it. In his introduction, again a text that has assumed an importance in its own right, Rorty said a good deal about how pragmatists are able to bypass some of the traditional issues associated with 'truth', a topic that receives scant attention in *Philosophy and the Mirror of Nature*. He also puts some meat on the skeletal accounts he gave of his three designated heroes: Dewey, Heidegger and Wittgenstein. The impression gained from reading these essays, and indeed Rorty's other essays, is that his philosophical career progressed much more smoothly than the 'tripartite' account suggests. If there was a break in the overall continuum, it came when he gained the confidence we referred to above and started to practise the relatively autonomous approach to philosophical discussion and enquiry first displayed in *Contingency, Irony, and Solidarity*.

Pragmatism

'Pragmatism' is a vague, ambiguous, and overworked word. Nevertheless, it names the chief glory of our country's intellectual tradition.   (Richard Rorty, *Consequences of Pragmatism*)

As we have repeatedly said before, Rorty was not only one of the key players in the recent revival of interest in pragmatism in general, but also a founder of the New Pragmatism. Hence, it may seem surprising that we have not yet discussed this aspect of his career. However, the explanation is quite straightforward. It has two strands to it. And, we need to distinguish between pragmatism and the New Pragmatism.

The first strand concerns the role that pragmatism plays in Rorty's major published works, leaving aside his essays. This role is sometimes minimal, sometimes self-effacing and rarely self-advertising. In *Philosophy and the Mirror of Nature*, pragmatism has no more than an honorific presence, somewhat in line with that of Dewey, Heidegger and Wittgenstein. A glance at the index will show, for example, that the philosopher Gilbert Ryle merits more attention than pragmatism. In *Contingency, Irony, and Solidarity*, pragmatism is nigh on invisible. Some essays pay more detailed attention to pragmatism, but, for the most part, they do not attempt to outline a unique pragmatist position.[9] Often, Rorty simply made very general allusions to the writings of classic pragmatists, especially James and Dewey, without working that material up into hard and fast principles or theoretical claims. Here is a typical example:

> For the pragmatists (among whom I number myself) the traditional questions of metaphysics and epistemology can be neglected because they have no social utility. It is not that they are devoid of meaning, nor that they rest on false premises; it is simply that the vocabulary of metaphysics and epistemology is of no practical use. (2007: 37–8)

What is the significance of all this?

The answer comes in the shape of our second strand. This involves the New Pragmatism, which we earlier tagged as 'postanalytic pragmatism'. Such Pragmatism is 'postanalytic' not in the sense that it comes *after* or *replaces* analytic philosophy, but rather in the sense that it defines its philosophical identity *independently* of that tradition. It is the kind pragmatism that, unlike its progenitor, ceases to allow itself to be defined by the concerns of the analytic tradition. It is, as we said in Chapter 2, autonomous. Recall, too, that the classic pragmatists, especially James and Dewey, spent a great deal of their time arguing with their peers and deflecting the criticisms of philosophers such as Russell and Moore. In many ways, as we indicated earlier, this was a mistake because it enabled the enemies of pragmatism to decide the terms of the debate and to fight their battles with it on their own territory. Rorty identified this mistake, whether consciously or otherwise, and avoided it.[10] Hence, when he talked about 'pragmatism', he was usually talking about the New Pragmatism, something that derives from classic pragmatism to the extent that it tends to substitute plain conceptions of practical utility (which include 'what helps us cope', 'what assuages our pain', 'what is of most interest to us' and 'what we find it best to do in the circumstances') for the abstract, highly theoretical constructs that philosophy has generally preferred. This New Pragmatism, postanalytic pragmatism, has the courage and imagination to strike out on its own. It no longer holds itself answerable to the philosophical tradition from which it diverges.[11]

Hence, when Rorty was actually *doing* philosophy, much of the terminology of classic pragmatism, terminology that made the kinds of references deemed necessary at the time to traditional philosophical topics such as 'knowledge', 'experience' and 'truth', fell by the wayside. The New Pragmatism no longer needs to keep reminding itself that it is a form of 'pragmatism'; it can just get on with the job of exploring issues of interest. It is for this reason that, when he was not deploying a framework of ideas to make things safer for it, Rorty often wrote extensively without pausing to explicitly invoke the name of the New Pragmatism.

This reason was supplemented by the fact that in his later essays Rorty was inclined to merge pragmatism with what he called cultural politics. By invoking this form of politics, he was able to substitute a socialized form of objectivity for its traditional ontological version, thereby encouraging philosophers to focus on discussing practical criteria of success rather than platonic questions about the ultimate constituents and nature of reality. In doing this, he came close to the anti-ontological position that Hilary Putnam adopted quite late in his own career (see EWO).

It is not easy to assess Rorty's accomplishments at this stage because a large part of his project involved challenging the current standards for such assessments. We have shown that at least some of the controversy about Rorty will die down when his work is read more carefully. For then the sharp divisions in his work will be smoothed out. The more homogeneous Rorty that emerges from this process is still likely to enrage traditionalists. But he will have triumphed on his own terms if he has persuaded history not to judge him according to their criteria. Whether he has surpassed Proust by creating the taste by which he is judged rather than simply that 'by which he judges himself' is for history to decide. If that decision is favourable, history will take a practical view of Rorty's achievements, paying tribute to the way in which he has opened up philosophical discussion, encouraged philosophers to cross the analytic–continental philosophy divide, introduced new or marginalized authors into the canon and stimulated debate in diverse areas including law, feminism, literary theory and even accountancy. On that score, he should be judged very kindly indeed. In Chapter 6 we discuss the vigorous and wide-ranging role that Rorty played in some of these areas and we show how he was putting New Pragmatists' ideas to work even when he was not openly announcing this.

4

PUTNAM'S CONTRIBUTIONS

I hope to convince you that pragmatism offers something far
better than the unpalatable alternatives which seem to be the
only possibilities today, both philosophically and politically.

(Hilary Putnam, *Pragmatism: An Open Question*)

Hilary Putnam is a prolific and influential philosopher who has had a
long and distinguished academic career. In his case, we do not need to
fill in as much background detail as we did with Rorty. For, although
Putnam has never been afraid of courting controversy, his philosophical career has been much more conventional that Rorty's.[1] As a result,
his views have not been inordinately clouded or distorted by the fog
of public notoriety.

Putnam's contributions to the growth of the New Pragmatism
have spanned some thirty years or so. During this lengthy period,
Putnam's overall position has been revised a number of times, and
to the extent that more recently, as James Conant has pointed out,
he has "become increasingly disenchanted with putting forward new
philosophical 'positions' of his own" (in Putnam 1995b: xii). Given
Putnam's deep dissatisfaction with the reductive aspects of overly
abstract or narrowly technical approaches to philosophical issues,
his eventual adoption of what we might call a 'positionless position' might, with hindsight, look inevitable. And no doubt this has
some bearing on how we should view his relationship to the New

Pragmatism. However, there is another sense in which his philosophical direction has never wavered.

He has travelled away from what he regards as the dubious metaphysics of traditional forms of realism. This metaphysics is epitomized by the notion of a mind-independent world, one that supposedly lies waiting beneath what James memorably termed the "man-made wrappings", one whose true nature is completely separate from our various notions of it. But, Putnam embarked on this journey while still wanting to hold on to what he takes to be of practical importance in realism and while still looking for "a way to do justice to our sense that knowledge claims are responsible to reality without recoiling into metaphysical fantasy" (POQ: 4). Along the way, he began to consistently invoke pragmatism as perhaps the best available option for setting aside the metaphysics of realism while retrieving what is useful about realism itself.

As a result, Putnam has become an astute commentator on the work of both James and Dewey, distilling from their texts a wealth of historically underwritten insights that help inform his own advocacy of a more open-minded and practical approach to philosophy in general. He has also assembled a wealth of his own texts that either deal directly with pragmatism or engage with related themes. For present purposes, although we will occasionally refer to other works, we shall concentrate on the following combination of books and articles: *Pragmatism: An Open Question* (1995a); "James's Theory of Truth" (R. A. Putnam 1997: 162–85); "The Question of Realism" (Putnam 1995b: 295–312); *Ethics without Ontology* (2004); "Education for Democracy" (Putnam & Putnam 1995b); and "Dewey's *Logic*" (Putnam & Putnam 1995a).

Putnam's multiple revisions of his philosophical outlook have been dominated by the issue of 'realism', as we just implied. His main objective in tackling this issue has been to steer clear of the philosophical excesses of either scepticism or idealism on the one hand and dogmatic realism on the other. According to scepticism, we can never prove that what passes for knowledge in our hands has its counterpart in the real world. This is intended to raise awkward doubts as to whether knowledge is even possible. Idealism holds that our capacity for knowledge cannot extend beyond the confines of our own minds or the one big mind that they form a part of. And, dogmatic realism claims we are entitled to assert certain things are real even though we may be unable to justify such an assertion in the strictest philosophical terms. This sort of realist does not try to satisfy the sceptic's demands for proof but rather refuses to accept their legitimacy or simply ignores them. Granted the amount of time and energy Putnam has devoted to avoiding these options rather than simply ditching realism altogether, it is not surprising that his handling of pragmatism embodies what we just alluded to as a 'retrievalist' element: that he tries to reclaim and preserve what he takes to be *its* realist element. This inclination to preserve what is valuable in classic pragmatism is one example of Putnam's general tendency to avoid what he calls 'the besetting sin of philosophers':

> The besetting sin of philosophers seems to be throwing the baby out with the bathwater. From the beginning each 'new wave' of philosophy has simply ignored the insights of the previous wave in the course of advancing its own … I want to urge that we attempt to understand, and to the extent that it is humanely possible overcome, the pattern of 'recoil' that causes philosophy to leap from frying pan to fire, from fire to a different frying pan, from different frying pan to a different fire, and so on apparently without end. (1995b: xiii)

In this cautionary sense, he departs from Rorty. For Rorty is much more concerned to leave old forms of philosophy behind than to try to rescue what is worthwhile in them. He sees pragmatism as a valuable vehicle for carrying philosophy forwards in this unburdened way. At the same time, and perhaps for the very reason of these differences with Rorty, Putnam may help provide a more immediately accessible defence of the New Pragmatism against critics who claim that it provides dubious refuge for relativists and other philosophical rogues who stubbornly refuse to face up to reality.

All of a piece with his approach to problems concerning realism, Putnam has also devoted much attention to the fact–value distinction, favouring the pragmatists' inclination to deny that there is any genuine dichotomy here, even implying, at times, that facts dissolve into values. This sets the scene for his holistic contention that there are no deep, philosophically significant, differences between scientific and ethical practices. In claiming this, he comes close to Rorty's view that the various realms of enquiry are seamlessly connected within the continuum of language, that they differ only in the type of tools they employ and the practical results they seek to achieve.

Putnam's role

Against this background Putnam's role in paving the way for the New Pragmatism can be broken down into four parts:

1. He has challenged received negative views of classic pragmatism by returning to the original texts in order to show how early critics especially tended to misread them.
2. He has taken some classic pragmatist views, for example James's much maligned views on truth, and shown how, when suitably modified, they stand up well against more recent alternatives.
3. He has advocated a thoroughgoing holism that traces back to James's work and from there embraces what he finds convincing in the relevant writings of Quine and Davidson.
4. He has insightfully explored the ways in which pragmatism can help resolve current difficulties in ethics, education and politics. In this way, he has relaunched the kind of ambitious classic pragmatist agenda for social improvement that was stalled by the barrage of early criticism.

Each of these is well worth considering in turn. But in each case, also, an issue we need to ponder, and one we will eventually need to confront, is: how is it that Putnam is thereby contributing to the New Pragmatism rather than simply helping create an intellectual climate that is now more hospitable to the original ideas of the classic pragmatists? For, given his conservatism in comparison to Rorty, the general question as to why Putnam's approach to philosophy is closer to that of New Pragmatism rather than the old pragmatism is a good one.

Interpreting classic pragmatism for present purposes

Once it was taken out of Peirce's more scientific hands,[2] pragmatism appeared to be vulnerable to some basic objections that, as we claimed in Chapter 2, early critics such as Russell and Moore made the most of.

Rorty, as we also noted, suggested that it is best to simply ignore this awkward phase in pragmatism's development. He believed that both the objections in question and the inclination to respond to them were ill-conceived: the product of a disposable perception of the nature of philosophy, a perception that pragmatism lacked the self-understanding, and perhaps will, to eschew at the time. Putnam, however, is more circumspect. He thinks it is well worth taking time out to set the record straight, to show that James and, to a lesser extent, Dewey *already* possessed the requisite self-knowledge but were unable to capitalize on this because their writings were treated so unfairly by their enemies. In this way, Putnam is again more circumspect than Rorty, and closer in general outlook to the classic pragmatists.

Putnam has now devoted a considerable amount of effort, often in collaboration with his wife Ruth Anna Putnam, to resurrecting some of James's and Dewey's philosophical views in order to show that they were frequently badly misconstrued. However, his approach is perhaps best illustrated in his 'Lesione italiane' lectures delivered in Rome in March 1992, and published in 1995 as *Pragmatism: An Open Question*. There, one of his goals is to partly substantiate his assessment of James as "a powerful thinker, as powerful as any in the last century" (POQ: 6), someone who was grossly underestimated by many of his philosophical peers. Already, we can once more see how Putnam's approach differs from Rorty's. Putnam is more appreciative of the classic pragmatists on their own terms, taken straight, as it were, independently of the accretions of critical rumour and innuendo. By contrast, when Rorty probed beneath these accruals, he often felt obliged to put some spin on what he discovered.

Putnam's strategy is candidly robust in that he starts with what is probably the hardest case: James's much maligned account of truth. And the passage he selects to demonstrate how that account has been misconstrued and, as a result, underestimated is one that was scornfully censured by Russell and then later tended to crop up whenever other critics wanted a quick and dirty way of dispensing with the idea that pragmatism represented a serious intellectual option.

Russell famously quoted James as saying: "The 'true' is only the expedient in the way of our thinking ... in the long run and on the whole of course" (1945: 817). And Putnam rightly contends that, in singling out this passage, Russell started something of a careless tradition in interpreting James and, indeed, pragmatism itself.

In this case, James is taken to be explicitly claiming on behalf of pragmatism that if the consequences of believing something are beneficial to human beings then that belief must be true; or, as Russell himself, with customary celerity, puts it, "A belief is 'true' when its effects are good" (POQ: 9). Putnam finds two major problems with this. First, it fails to capture what James was trying to say: his 'intended meaning'. And secondly, it does not accurately report what James actually said. Here is the original passage from which Russell made what Putnam regards as an all too convenient extraction:

> 'The true', to put it very briefly, is only the expedient in the way of our thinking, just as 'the right' is only the expedient in the way of our behaving. Expedient in almost any fashion; expedient in the long run and on the whole of course, for what meets expediently all the experience in sight won't necessarily meet all further experiences satisfactorily. Experience, as we know, has ways of *boiling over*, and making us correct our present formulas.
>
> (PMT: 106)

Putnam says Russell ignores the plethora of qualifications here. And, he suggests, contrary to Russell's interpretation, these provide "obvious indications that what we have is a thematic statement, and not an attempt to formulate a definition of 'true'" (POQ: 9). Furthermore, Putnam argues that Russell compounds this basic error by first conjuring up his own absurdly reductive notion of 'expediency' and then foisting it on James. At this point, Putnam remarks with some obvious irritation, "all possibility of understanding what James is actually saying vanishes!" (*ibid.*).

Putnam's exasperation is understandable. For James never subscribed to a univocal conception of expediency. Indeed, in the very text Russell refers to he takes pains to distinguish different types of statements and asserts that they require corresponding differences in the kind of expediency that ensures their truth. Thus factual statements, particularly scientific ones, are best evaluated according to their predictive utility. When we take into account other criteria of expediency such as conservation of established doctrine, simplicity and general coherence – "What fits every part of life best and combines with the collectivity of experience's demands, nothing being omitted" (1998: 44) – it is clear that James's position is far more sophisticated than Russell seems prepared to take the trouble to imply.

To make things even worse, Putnam tells us, Russell actively encouraged "the view often attributed to James – that a statement is true if it will make people subjectively happy to believe it" (POQ: 9). Unfortunately, it is only a small step from this kind of attribution to the full-blooded subjectivism all too frequently set up as a target by other impatient critics who jibe that 'true' for a pragmatist amounts to 'true for me'. All this flies in the face of the subtlety and complexity of James's approach. He has no time for the notion of equating truth with any narrow or otherwise simplistic conception of psychological satisfaction. Indeed, 'true for me' is simply not part of his philosophical lexicon. In his much broader account, satisfaction "is no abstract satisfaction *überhaupt*, felt by an unspecified being, but is assumed to consist of such satisfactions (in the plural) as concretely existing men actually do find in their beliefs" (PMT: 270). These are many. But, one example, the satisfaction found in consistency, is sufficient to highlight the inadequacy of the narrow subjectivist objection:

> Above all we find *consistency* satisfactory, consistency between our present idea and the entire rest of our mental equipment, including the whole order of our sensations, and that of our intuitions of likeness and difference, and our whole stock of previously acquired truths. (*Ibid.*: 271)

The truth of particular claims is to be assessed according to their relationship to reality as it shows its face by making practical differences across the whole repertoire of human mental life, the kind of life that, as Putnam aptly reminds us, functions as part and parcel of a *community* of beings. It is not confined to the heads of particular individuals, and has little to do with individual happiness. Furthermore, individuals do not have a free hand in this respect. They cannot act on matters of truth evaluation without encountering epistemic resistance from without:

> Pent in, as the pragmatist more than anyone else sees himself to be, between the whole body of funded truths squeezed from the past and the coercions of the world of sense about him, who so well as he feels the immense pressure of objective control under which our minds perform their operations?   (PMT: 112–13)

Putnam's own project of revisiting the texts of classic pragmatism in this way has been supported by numerous other projects of a similar kind. Tom Burke, for example, has shown in some detail how Russell "misunderstood several concepts and distinctions which are fundamental to Dewey's views" and was therefore ill-suited to judge Dewey's account of logic (Burke 1998: ix). And, in an insightful assessment of James's early British critics, Timothy Sprigge argues that Moore and Russell in particular failed to grasp what James was trying to do (Sprigge 2004). Although such ventures gain their credence from the hitherto unacknowledged virtues of the original texts, much of the impetus behind them also comes from a quasi-sociological source: the phenomenon we referred to as 'philosophical celebrity power' in the Introduction. The fact that well-established and highly acclaimed philosophers such as Putnam and Rorty were taking the classic pragmatists very seriously encouraged other thinkers to take a closer look at their work. What they saw, through fresh eyes, then often reflected badly on received views of pragmatism's philosophical worth.[3]

Making substantive views more acceptable: truth

> One can, I believe, learn a great deal from James.
> (Hilary Putnam, *Pragmatism: An Open Question*)

As well as trying to show that the classic pragmatists' writings were often treated shoddily by their early critics, Putnam also attempts to place some of the substantive views involved in a better light by contemporary standards. Once again, James's account of truth provides a good example of this.

Although he called truth a "ticklish subject" (PMT: 95), James could equally have termed it 'provocative'. Peirce's 'idealized' approach, according to which truth is what turns out to be undeniable when enquiry has run its course, attracted some critical attention. But, James's own account, partly derived from Peirce but also from Schiller and Dewey, provoked the dramatically hostile reaction that scarred classic pragmatism for a long period and still, at times, threatens to do the same to the New Pragmatism.

Putnam's approach to James's account of truth is both complex and sophisticated. He does not commit himself to James's position, and nor does he deflect actual and potential criticism of that position by trying to substantiate its main arguments. His aim is rather first to give James a fair hearing, as we saw above, and then to show that there are very useful elements in his views, even if those views fall short of a tidy and completely defensible conception of truth. What Putnam finds especially useful in James's views is something that he values in classic pragmatism in general: the 'primacy of practice'. And in this connection, he reminds us that "the classical pragmatists do not believe that there is a 'first philosophy' higher than practice that we take most seriously when the chips are down" (1995b: 154).

Putnam recounts that, for explanatory purposes, James insisted on linking truth to practical methods of confirmation. If we deal with truth on these terms, says Putnam, this will also enable us to dissolve some of the mystification generally associated with the idea of 'correspondence'. We need to take seriously

> the point that James insisted on, that our grasp of the notion of truth must not be represented as simply a mystery mental act by which we relate ourselves to a relation called 'correspondence' totally independent of the practices by which we *decide* what is and is not true.   (POQ: 11)

Putnam sees it as both practically useful and philosophically important here that James's approach allows us to keep a realist vocabulary in play without making ourselves dependent on the traditional metaphysical interpretation of that vocabulary. That is, we can continue to speak, as James is more than happy to, and even says we surely *must*, of true claims being 'true of reality'.[4] And we can even concur with the literary critic James Wood's stark insistence that "realism is not a law, but a lenient tutor, for it schools its own truants" (Wood 2002: 167). But, we can do so because we recognize this as *common-sense talk*, the kind of talk that does not necessarily fare well if it is philosophically upgraded.[5] When we try to make the notion of 'correspondence', for instance, carry intellectual weight, it lets us down. We soon lose sight of what it is supposed to mean. While it works well enough for purposes of ordinary discourse, it becomes opaque when it is allocated a hefty philosophical role.

In the face of what might seem to be the natural sceptical rejoinder that perhaps this very failure reflects badly on the original way of speaking, that such 'common-sense talk' must be suspect if it crashes when launched at any philosophical height, James suggests we reverse the moral. We should ditch not that way of speaking but rather the higher level, theoretical reification of its concepts and, most importantly, the narrowly confined philosophical picture that encourages such reification. In this picture, notions such as 'correspondence' and 'agreement' are reduced to quasi-primitive status (as in 'our beliefs are true only when they correspond to reality'). They thereby carry little explanatory weight. Whereas the picture that James wants to encourage, and the one that Putnam finds more attractive, involves what we might call a 'pragmatic expansion' of these same notions, enabling them to be cashed out in all sorts of practical ways. James contends that it thus "converts the absolutely empty notion of a static relation of 'correspondence' between our minds and reality into that of a rich and active commerce" (PMT: 39). James is quite frank about the overall contrast in approaches here:

> The pragmatizing epistemologist posits there a reality and a mind with ideas. What now, he asks, can make those ideas true of that reality? Ordinary epistemology contents itself with the vague statement that the ideas must 'correspond' or 'agree'; the pragmatist insists on being more concrete, and asks what such 'agreement' may mean in detail.   (PMT: 98)[6]

In the end, Putnam finds fault with James's account of truth,[7] but he holds it up for closer examination as an example of how to think about this whole topic in richer, and potentially more fruitful, ways. It is in this sense that Putnam believes James's view on truth stand up well against more recent alternatives.

Holism

Holism is basically the view that things cannot be philosophically explained or understood in isolation. Different kinds of holism derive from the nature of the 'things' in question. Hence Quine is famous for espousing a form of what we might call 'confirmation holism', as characterized by his famous contention that "statements about the external world face the tribunal of experience not individually, but as a corporate body" (1953b: 27), and Davidson advocated a related semantic holism of belief, maintaining that the truth of beliefs cannot be determined atomistically: their veracity leans on that of a cluster of other beliefs. I cannot believe that the tree in my garden is an oak, without at least tacitly believing a host of other things concerning the nature of trees, gardens and so forth. Refusal to endorse a sufficient number of complementary beliefs of this kind casts serious doubt as to whether words like 'tree' and 'garden' actually mean anything in my mouth.

In *Pragmatism: An Open Question*, Putnam claims that holism is "one of the chief characteristics of James's philosophy" (POQ: 7). Here, he says he is chiefly referring to its denial of "many familiar dualisms" (*ibid.*). And, he goes on to argue that one of the great virtues of this aspect of James's pragmatism is that it treats fact, value and theory as "interpenetrating and interdependent" (*ibid.*). By returning to the holistic theme in James's work, Putnam opens up some interesting historical issues regarding the extent to which this work pre-dated or influenced the later holism of philosophers such as Quine and Davidson. These issues are beyond the scope of this book. More important for our purposes is the fact that Putnam finds it necessary to go back as far as James.

For it seems he feels compelled to go there because James's holism was more thoroughgoing, and in a sense more radical than later versions. This makes it a useful source of inspiration for someone, like

Putnam himself, who is looking for ideas that will help find a way past some of the major difficulties bequeathed by the analytic tradition.

Recall that Putnam is searching for a path that takes us beyond "familiar dualisms – fact and value, fact and theory, fact and interpretation" (POQ: 13).[8] For someone in this position, James's writings can be a revelation. Holism is all pervasive. Of course James himself did not use the term 'holism', but with hindsight that is now the best word for the 'interconnectedness' that dominates much of his philosophy and, in particular, his accounts of the confirmation of truth claims, the nature of experience and the relationship between the individual and the world – and, indeed, the way in which these accounts are seamlessly woven together (see Malachowski 2010b).

In the case of 'comfirmation', for example, James replaces the seemingly simple, but actually mysterious, correspondence model in which empirical truth claims are confirmed according to whether they match up with how things are in the world with a much more complex picture in which a claim to truth is acceptable if it "fits every part of life best and combines with the collectivity of experience's demands, nothing being omitted" (PMT: 44). Notice that this is even more radical than Quinean holism. According to one of Quine's well-known formulations, the unit of confirmation for a sentence expressing an empirical claim is the whole of science. For James, it is the whole of life!

The practical relevance of pragmatism

In my case, turning to American pragmatism does not mean turning to a metaphysical theory.
(Hilary Putnam, *Pragmatism: An Open Question*)

Philosophy recovers itself when it ceases to be a device for dealing with the problems of philosophers and becomes a method, cultivated by philosophers, for dealing with the problems of men. (John Dewey, *Reconstruction in Philosophy*)

Although he is not in favour of abandoning the generally accepted standards of intellectual rigour in argumentation that characterize the analytic tradition in philosophy, Putnam has increasingly turned away from that tradition and towards pragmatism. And, he has done this because he has become more and more concerned with the general question as to what it means to live a good life, and hence with the practical difference philosophy can make in that regard.[9] The Jamesian themes we have discussed so far in this chapter still have some close connections with the abstract themes of analytic philosophers. There is a sense in which, even though his ideas point to possibilities for philosophizing beyond it, James still spoke from within the analytic tradition. Nevertheless, Putnam assures us that he find James important because of James's abiding interest in the question of how we should live:

> We want ideals and we want a world view, and we want our ideals and our world view to support one another. Philosophy which is all argument feeds no real hunger; while philosophy which is all vision feeds a real hunger but it feeds it pabulum [i.e. 'food for the mind']. If there is one overriding reason for being concerned with James's thought, it is that he was a genius who was concerned with real hungers, and whose thought, whatever its shortcomings, provides substantial food for thought – and not just for thought, but for life.   (POQ: 22–3)

Putnam's interest in the practical relevance of pragmatism, has an even clearer and more direct pay-off when he discusses the writings of Dewey, someone who had moved into the territory James pointed towards.[10]

In these writings, Putnam finds a rich source of ideas for exploring practical solutions to problems in ethics, education and democracy, and in ways that are not circumscribed by the traditional approaches of analytic philosophers. But, ever mindful of pragmatism's bad philosophical press, he is careful to clarify "that 'practical problems' here means simply 'problems we encounter in practice,' specific and situated problems, as opposed to abstract, idealized, or theoretical problems" (EWO: 28).

Ethics

In the case of ethics, Putnam finds support in Dewey's work for an approach that deals with ethical problems immediately without first trying to cut them down to a theoretically convenient size. 'Immediately' has multiple connotations here. It conveys an appropriate sense of 'directness', of philosophy confronting ethical problems without the intermediary of theoretical considerations. There is also an implied sense of urgency: the problems in question require practical solution now – they do not simply constitute the raw materials for an ongoing, overarching theoretical project that seeks to pin down general principles for resolving such problems once and for all times. And, this urgency also signals the fact that ethical problems are time-bound: that they involve "specific problems faced by human beings in given cultural circumstances" (EWO: 31). Recognition of the ways in which ethical predicaments are located in time is something that Dewey extrapolated from his early studies of Hegel and then put the kind of practical complexion on that attracts philosophers like Putnam who are trying to move beyond the view that such predicaments can be ironed out by the construction of timeless theory alone.

The notion that ethical problems need to be addressed as practical difficulties particular to a time and place has implications for the ambitions of philosophers. They need no longer seek to identify the absolute theoretical justification for moral imperatives that should govern the behaviour of all human beings for eternity. By the same token, they need not aim for infallibility in matters of ethics. Putnam instructively sums up these 'implications' as follows:

> If philosophers can contribute to a reasoned resolution of some of the problems of his or her time, that is no small achievement, and that some of her assumptions will in future no doubt have to be qualified or even rejected is only to be expected. Our task as philosophers isn't to achieve 'immortality' ... If we can improve the way we deal with specific evils, with the hunger and violence and inequality that mar our world, we need not be disappointed if we cannot distill out from our dealings a textbook of universal ethical truths that will infallibly guide all future generations.
>
> (*Ibid.*: 31–2)

Education and politics in general

The educational point of view enables one to envisage the philosophical problems where they arise and thrive, where they are at home, and where acceptance or rejection makes a difference in practice. If we are willing to conceive education as the process of forming fundamental dispositions, intellectual and emotional, philosophy may be defined as the general theory of education.

(John Dewey, *Democracy and Education*)

Dewey had huge influence on education, and not just in America, but worldwide. He is commonly associated with the preponderance of progressive methods, and often unfairly blamed for their excesses. In fact, Dewey was critical of loose-limbed, ill-disciplined approaches, believing that, as he expressed it in *Education and Experience*, "the ideal aim of education is creation of the power of self-control" (quoted in Putnam 1995b: 227). He further believed that educational thinking had been infected by an 'either/or' mentality of which 'either traditional or progressive' was a prime example. And, as Putnam rightly reminds us, he actually tried to steer a path between "the extremes of authoritarian traditionalism and undirected progressivism" (*ibid.*: 221).

Putnam is interested in Dewey's views on education for more general reasons than the light they may shed on the traditionalist–progressive debate *within* the field of education as such. Indeed, these reasons are pragmatic. He wants to use those views to help clarify practical issues regarding multiculturalism and, by extension, the nature of modern democratic societies. Putman's interest is thus, in the end, primarily *political*.

This motivation chimes well with Dewey's own approach to education. He did not consider it to be an independent topic. Following Hegel, he took education to be a societal phenomenon: "the method by which civil society reproduces itself" (*ibid.*: 225). More precisely, Dewey held that education is society's method not just of reproducing itself, but also of regenerating itself in improved forms. Educated citizens are better able to participate in civil life. They are also better able to stand back from it sufficiently to see what is of value in it and how it can be enhanced.

75

Moreover, Dewey contended that educational life ought to blend into 'civil life', and hence politics, in two important senses. First, children should be taught in ways that place greater emphasis on the development of 'reflective intelligence' within a communal setting. This fits in with his idea that the pursuit of knowledge is essentially a *co-operative* venture, one in which views are tested for efficacy against shared experience and a pool of practical know-how. This kind of education eases the transition from life within the school community to that within the community at large.[11] School life is civil life in miniature. Furthermore, Dewey argued that there should be no abrupt division between school activities and those pursued later. Proper education involves a continuous process of enquiry and consequent self-improvement, one that carries on throughout the whole of life. For, as Dewey once put it, "the aim of education is to enable individuals to continue their education" (DE: 100).

How does Putnam connect all this with 'multiculturalism' and the nature of democracy? The connection is not difficult for him to forge precisely because of the twofold blending of educational and civil life that we just referred to.

After discussing how Dewey and his followers "lost the battle for multiculturalism" after the First World War because of "a wave of post-war chauvinism" (1995b: 222), Putnam revisits Dewey's case for 'pluralism' to see whether it can illuminate the issues that are now associated with multiculturalism. In doing so, as he himself tells us, he is looking for "the resources to transcend the Eurocentric/ Multicultural dichotomy" (*ibid.*: 223).

This dichotomy will be overcome, Putnam argues, when citizens show not only respect for one another's cultural backgrounds, but also a willingness to acquire more knowledge about those backgrounds, the kind of knowledge that fosters understanding of beliefs, experiences and values that might otherwise appear to be inexplicably alien. The reciprocity involved here, the mutuality of the respect and understanding, is what is supposed to transcend the dichotomy. And, the resources that Putnam finds in Dewey's work for helping society to move towards such reciprocity include, most importantly, his 'experimental' approach to values and his conception of human identity as something that is forged through cooperative activity within an appropriate community rather than simply given. Clearly, the strong continuities that Dewey believes should exist between school life and civil life imply that experimentation with values and self-creation has to be a vital part of the educational process. In discussing the benefits of a Deweyan approach to current problems associated with multiculturalism, Putnam puts great emphasis on a fallible practical process of cooperation between different parties who try to discover common cultural ground without thereby suppressing diversity. He regards this as far more promising than any attempt to theorize such problems away by identifying abstract general principles that all such parties should ideally subscribe to.

Democracy, identity and knowledge

> The only way to prepare for social life is to engage in social life. (John Dewey, *Democracy and Education*)

An emphasis on the practical side of things continues when Putnam draws on Dewey's writings to explore the nature of democracy. Dewey maintained that democracy is not just one political system out of an array of possible alternatives. He believed that there is something special about democracy, something that makes it the natural choice for human communities. Dewey even went as far as to imply that there is a necessary connection between the notion of democracy and that of community. Indeed, he claimed that democracy should be viewed as "the idea of community life itself" (DE: 27). There is a larger story behind this, one that involves Dewey's conception of human identity as something created, not given, something forged by human agency within social situations. We can foster our talents and establish who we are only by participating in social life: "human nature is developed only when its elements take part in directing things which are common, things for the sake of which men and women form groups – families, industrial companies, governments, churches, scientific associations, and so on" (DE: 33).[12]

Putnam does not explore the whole of this background story, but rather concentrates on one key aspect of what it is that Dewey thinks is special about democracy, namely that it provides the best means for communities to resolve the various difficulties they encounter.

Putnam paraphrases the reason for this as follows: "Democracy is not just one form of social life among other workable forms of social life; it is the precondition for the application of intelligence to the solution of social problems" (Putnam 1995b: 180).[13]

Democracy is a 'precondition' in this sense because it is the only general system of political organization that allows for, and indeed encourages, the free flow of information that enables citizens to put forward and criticize practical plans for resolving the kinds of problems that life within a complex community inevitably generates.[14] Putnam rightly points out that in this picture of democracy, social life is a process of continual experimentation, not in the sense of capriciously trying things on for size, but rather in the more serious Deweyan sense of positing practical suggestions for better ways of living together and testing them for results in the crucible of daily life.

Putnam narrows things down still further by highlighting the *epistemic* feature of what Dewey regards as special about democracy: it is the best kind of problem-solving system of social organization because it generates the conditions under which the appropriate knowledge can be acquired. This still leans heavily on Dewey's larger story, in which proper enquiry requires cooperative activity from engaged participants in social life rather than the distanced theorizing of 'spectators': "Knowledge cooped up in a private consciousness is a myth, and knowledge of social phenomena is peculiarly dependent upon dissemination, for only by distribution can such knowledge be either obtained or tested" (LW 2: 345). Once again however, rather than delving into the details of the larger picture, Putnam extrapolates an interesting line of argument from what he has identified as the special epistemic feature of democracy. Putnam believes that this argument provides an epistemological justification of democracy.

The very idea of such an argument raises some interesting issues. First, as Dewey's distinguished biographer Robert Westbrook points out, we can be pretty certain

> that Dewey never offered anything that he *called* 'an epistemological argument for democracy,' for 'epistemology' was a dirty word in Dewey's vocabulary. He blamed what he termed the 'epistemology industry' of modern philosophy since Descartes

for creating all the unsolvable problems that he wanted philosophy to stop trying to solve and simply get over.

(Westbrook 1998: 129)

Secondly, and following on from this, Putnam's apparent assumption that democracy needs, and can be provided with, such a 'justification' marks out one of the major differences in his approach to pragmatism from that of Rorty, who shared Dewey's distaste for epistemology and, indeed, for foundational projects in general. We shall deal with the first of these concerns now and defer discussion of Putnam's differences with Rorty until Chapter 5.

Although there is a question mark over the term 'epistemological' in the title of the argument Putnam extracts from his writings, the argument itself is not completely foreign to Dewey's approach. Indeed, Westbrook suggests that when we abandon the term and substitute 'logical', leaving us with a 'logical argument for democracy', then we come much closer to something that Dewey might have been willing to endorse even if he did not explicitly advocate it. For, as Westbrook explains, Putnam links the argument "principally to Dewey's theory of inquiry, that is his logic", and "logic was where he lodged his constructive efforts to write about knowledge, meaning, and truth after he himself got over the problems of epistemology" (*ibid.*: 129–30). The logical argument for democracy has three main components.[15] The first involves Dewey's claim that the best way for human beings to acquire and sustain true beliefs – or 'warranted assertions' in his terminology – is by means of the various methods, practices and values of a community of competent enquirers. In such a community, doubt is an entirely practical matter: something stimulated by the consequences of failure, or some form of breakdown, among the settled host of beliefs acquired by well-established, community-wide, procedures. Under the impetus of such a stimulus, the community of enquirers subjects its methods and practices to further enquiry. And, the second element of the argument, the enquiry extends to cover value judgements. This is important for precisely the reason Westbrook identifies: "It is the application of inquiry to value-laden 'problematic situations' that makes inquiry available for the sorts of issues that are most likely to confront social and political communities" (*ibid.*: 131). Finally, and this is the crux of the overall argument, such methods of belief acquisition and the kind of 'further enquiry' that protects the integrity of these methods over time can only flourish in a democratic community. Putnam makes this final claim on grounds that he calls 'cognitive'. These involve three features that characterize democracy and are necessary for the acquisition of problem-solving knowledge: (i) the unhindered flow of information; (ii) the personal freedom to pursue enquiry to wherever it leads; and (iii) the inclusion of diverse parties. The third characteristic is important because it allows for what we might call 'social epistemic competency': the needs and problems of a community are best known by its members rather than some exclusive elite. And here, Putnam relies on Dewey's *The Public and Its Problems*, in which he makes a case for wider participation in the formulation of public policy. Dewey claims that only the members of the relevant community know where the shoe of social life pinches: that, as Westbrook puts it, "without the participation of the public in the formulation of such policy, it could not reflect the common needs and interests of society". And, it could not reflect these "because these needs and interests were known only to the public" (*ibid.*: 131).[16]

Westbrook evinces two persuasive conclusions about this 'logical argument for democracy': first, on matters of interpretation, it is an argument that Dewey could have made even though he did not, and secondly, on matters of substance, it "is vulnerable to criticism at every step in its progression" (*ibid.*: 137). At first blush, the latter is quite disconcerting, but as we now move on to summarize Putnam's contribution to the New Pragmatism, the 'vulnerability' it mentions will perhaps seem less perturbing.

Putnam and the New Pragmatism

We have discussed various ways in which Putnam has prepared the way for a sympathetic reassessment of the classic pragmatism of James and Dewey, in particular. In essence, we have said that he has revisited the texts to help clear away entrenched misconceptions about them and show how they express ideas of current sociopolitical interest. But what has this to do with the New Pragmatism?

Putnam does not class himself as a card-carrying pragmatist, still less as a New Pragmatist. Of course, we should not expect him to answer to a name that has been coined for the purposes of this book.[17] But, that is beside the point. What matters is the causal effect that Putnam's work has had on the emergence of what we are calling the 'New Pragmatism'. These effects are threefold.

First, Putnam has indirectly encouraged the growth of the New Pragmatism by making the term 'pragmatism' itself seem less of a dirty philosophical word. He has helped to ensure that a New Pragmatist need not receive a hostile intellectual reception just because 'pragmatism' itself has such negative connotations. Since Putnam has an international reputation and wide-ranging interests, this factor also helps with the New Pragmatism's cosmopolitan aspirations. Secondly, Putnam has provided substantial first-hand evidence that one of the New Pragmatism's main ambitions is realistic. The ambition is to carry out, and further stimulate, forms of philosophical discourse that do not veer off into ineffectual abstraction or get sidetracked by interminable debates provoked by stale assumptions. This is the value of Putnam's Deweyan discussions of such topics as the fact–value distinction, multiculturalism and the nature of democracy. Irrespective of whether the arguments they contain are technically vulnerable, these discussions vividly illustrate that it is possible to say valuable things without going over and over the same old philosophical ground or recycling well-worn philosophical concepts and distinctions. Of course, the moratorium on 'vulnerability' comes at a price. The things so said need to be useful and interesting. This constraint is necessary; otherwise the point becomes trivial. It is easy enough to avoid traditional philosophical territory, as many do, by being ignorant of its existence or by simply failing to recognize its value and significance. Finally, we should again mention the 'celebrity effect' that we referred to earlier. The respect earned by Putnam's insightful labours has ensured that pragmatisms of all shapes and sizes and pragmatists of all persuasions stand a better chance of attracting attention from publishers, readers, students, conference and course organizers and even public figures such as politicians. The New Pragmatism has probably been the largest beneficiary of this effect.

5

PUTNAM AND RORTY: PRAGMATISM WITHOUT RECONCILIATION

Putnam thinks that my radical version of pragmatism gives rise to pointless paradoxes – that it saves us from the frying pan of what he calls "metaphysical realism" only to throw us into the fire of relativism.

(Richard Rorty, "Hilary Putnam and the Relativist Menace")

Putnam and Rorty argued with one another for over a period of about thirty years. That debate sheds some important light on the New Pragmatism. For it shows how the two thinkers most responsible for reviving interest in a pragmatist approach to philosophy diverged in their beliefs as to what that approach should involve. Furthermore, this disagreement is in many ways more instructive than those between the proponents of the New Pragmatism and their external critics. For these are always liable to deteriorate into the kind of sterile, energy-sapping contests that stifled classic pragmatism.

In this chapter, we shall review certain aspects of the debate,[1] including a number of the primary texts that it generated, and some of the related commentary. We then conclude that the New Pragmatism can thrive without reconciling all the differences between Putnam and Rorty. This in itself indicates the robust, self-critical and flexible nature of the New Pragmatism.

Difference despite agreement

There is an immediately apparent asymmetry in the Putnam–Rorty debate. Putnam maintains that Rorty's pragmatism is fundamentally flawed, and spends far more time trying to establish those flaws than in elucidating or revising his own views in response to Rorty's replies. Although respectful, he is, in essence, the attacker. Rorty, by contrast, played a more conciliatory and defensive role. While he was keen to amend Putnam's position, and was occasionally exasperated by it, he devoted most of his time to either clarifying his own approach to show why it was not vulnerable to Putnam's objections or modifying it in the light of those objections. The debate spans a wealth of writings by the two philosophers. Putnam is inclined to take a synoptic approach to issues, and when he does so he frequently refers, in passing, to his differences with Rorty. However, these differences are crystallized when both philosophers take time out to deal with them specifically. Some of the seminal texts in this respect are: "A Comparison of Something with Something Else'" (Putnam 1995d), "Richard Rorty on Reality and Justification" (Putnam 2000), *Realism with a Human Face* (Putnam 1990), "Solidarity or Objectivity" (Rorty 1991c), "Rorty Responds" (Rorty 2000b), "Hilary Putnam and the Relativist Menace" (Rorty 1998c) and "The Question of Realism" (Putnam 1995c). The penultimate work mentioned here is one we shall dip into to start with because it provides an excellent introduction to the features of the Putnam–Rorty debate that we want to focus on.

Rorty began by identifying five areas of wholehearted agreement with Putnam, the kind of agreement that aligns them against "a lot of other philosophers" (1998c: 43). He depicted them in Putnam's own words which are well worth quoting in full:

1. "Elements of what we call 'language' or 'mind' *penetrate so deeply into what we call 'reality' that the very project of representing ourselves as being 'mappers' of something 'language independent' is fatally compromised from the start.* Like Relativism, but in a different way, Realism is an impossible attempt to view the world from Nowhere" (Putnam 1990: 28).
2. "We should accept the position we are fated to occupy in any case, the position of beings who cannot have a view of the world

that does not reflect our interests and values, but who are, for all that, committed to regarding some views of the world – and, for that matter, some interests and values – as better than others" (*ibid.*: 178).

3. "What Quine called 'the indeteminacy of translation' should rather be viewed as the *interest relativity* of translation. 'Interest relativity' contrasts with *absoluteness*, not with objectivity. It can be objective that an interpretation or an explanation is the correct one, *given* the interests which are relevant in the context" (*ibid.*: 120).

4. "The heart of pragmatism, it seems to me – of James's and Dewey's pragmatism, if not of Peirce's – was the insistence on the supremacy of the agent's point of view. If we find that we must take a certain point of view, use a certain 'conceptual system', when we are engaged in practical activity, in the widest sense of 'practical activity, then we must not simultaneously advance the claim that it is not really 'the way things are in themselves'" (1987: 83).

5. "To say, as [Bernard] Williams sometimes does, that convergence to one big picture is required by the very concept of knowledge is sheer dogmatism … It is, indeed, the case that ethical knowledge cannot claim absoluteness; but that is because the notion of absoluteness is incoherent" (1990: 171).

Rorty then claimed that given the large measure of agreement manifested by such passages, he was puzzled as to "what keeps us apart" (1998b: 44). He was right to sense that Putnam feels there is a significant gap between them: on almost every occasion that he refers to Rorty, he points out a difference or takes care to distance himself from him. And Rorty was right to be perplexed. But, there is a common bone of contention here.

Rorty identified it immediately when he went on to say that he was puzzled "in particular about why Putnam thinks of me as a 'cultural relativist'" (*ibid.*). Putnam is anxious that Rorty's views on a cluster of notions that includes truth, justification and objectivity leave him open to such charges. And not only that, he thinks that Rorty's position is vulnerable to rather simplistic arguments to the effect that it is self-defeating. This is a mistake on Putnam's part. But, it is one that is made by many of Rorty's critics. In the latter instance, it is usually the result of a failure to read Rorty's writings carefully enough: exactly the kind of failure that the early critics of classic pragmatism were often guilty of. In Putnam's case it is a combination of that and a failure of pragmatist nerve. He is reluctant, or perhaps simply unable, to follow through on the full implications of the views he shares with Rorty.[2] Having said this, let us return to Rorty's own assessment of the situation before turning to that of some insightful commentators.

Rorty without relativism

> We pragmatists shrug off charges that we are 'relativists' or 'irrationalists' by saying that these charges presuppose precisely the distinctions we reject.
>
> (Richard Rorty, *Philosophy and Social Hope*)

Rorty's response to the charge of relativism was quite clear and unequivocal and he voiced it on many occasions. He was not, and never had been, a crude relativist of the 'anything goes' variety. Furthermore, nothing in his writings entailed that he was, even unwittingly. His philosophical views permitted him to judge particular truth claims or value statements and throw out the deficient ones accordingly. However, his gloss on the justification for making such judgements floated free of realist rhetoric. And, this means *philosophical* realist rhetoric: the kind of rhetoric intended to provide a deep explanation of what is really going on. Rorty could still speak with the vulgar: "Yes, there *really is* an elephant in the swimming pool right now". But, when pressed to give a philosophical explanation of the claims made in such speech he would forsake the metaphysics of depth and go horizontal by appealing to social considerations, the explanation of which did not presuppose acts of comparison between entities such as the sentence "Yes, there really is an elephant in the swimming pool right now", or the components thereof, and extra-linguistic counterparts.

On Rorty's view of things, his opponents were actually on far shakier ground than him, not least because of their self-deception regarding their own rhetoric. They spoke about him, and Putnam does this too, as if he were leaving an important metaphysical element out of his explanations by staying on the social surface. Whereas he felt they were in trouble when *they* were pressed on what digging deeper actually involves. For them, there was nowhere to go. They were stuck with lofty sounding appeals to reality 'as it is in its own right', and the like. But, there was no way for them to drop anchor outside language. Rather than taking up the metaphysical slack, their explanations provoked a philosophical mess. Compare two explanations as to why such and such a claim is true:

- Rorty's supposedly relativistic explanation: this claim is true because all the available evidence suggests it is true and my peers, including experts in the field, hold it to be true on the basis of the very same evidence. Furthermore, all social arrangements, including empirical predications, that have been made on the assumption this claim is true have worked out well so far and there seems to be no evidence to show that they will not continue to do so in the future.
- A rival philosophical explanation that supposedly picks up the metaphysical slack: this claim is true because it corresponds to how things are in the world.

The first explanation has plenty of scope for non-circular elaboration of the social factors involved. Furthermore, anyone who believed something on the sort of grounds it adduces would seem to be acting *rationally*[3] (indeed, the explanation appears to have normative power: in the specified circumstances, the claim in question *ought* to be believed and it would be irrational not to do so). By contrast, it is difficult to see how the second explanation can be expanded either non-circularly or without falling into philosophical mystification by resorting to primitives (i.e. words that cannot be defined in terms of other words – sorts of conceptual atoms, if you like). Indeed, it is difficult to see how it is much of an explanation at all. Nevertheless, it is the Rortyan kind of explanation that has provoked accusation of mindless relativism, irrationalism and so on. How can this be? The answer involves a convoluted history, one plausible narrative version of which was offered by Rorty in *Philosophy and the Mirror of Nature*.

But, if his account is right, if the philosophical views in question were stubbornly subscribed to because of the compelling attraction of underlying images and metaphors, then it should not, in fact, be surprising that the reasonableness of Rorty's own alternative picture should go unrecognized by many.

What the New Pragmatism needs to do is create new ways of saying philosophical things that are efficacious in practical terms and carry within them their own alternative modes of imagistic and metaphorical attraction. Building on Rorty's own attempts at this would be a good start.

Before we discuss why Putnam keeps company with critics who accuse Rorty of epistemological recklessness and then examine whether this is detrimental to the New Pragmatism, let us look at what some shrewd commentators have said about the issues at stake between Putnam and Rorty.

Rockwell: unavoidable questions and conceptual incoherencies

What lurks in the background of Putnam's criticisms of me is his dislike of, and my enthusiasm for, a picture of human beings as just complicated animals.

(Richard Rorty, *Philosophy and Social Hope*)

In his article "Rorty, Putnam and the Pragmatist View of Epistemology and Metaphysics", Teed Rockwell makes some intriguing radical claims – that the classic pragmatists believed metaphysics was indispensable and were right to do so, that analytic philosophy needs to learn "how to cure the *anti-metaphysical* disease which made its first appearance in the *Critique of Pure Reason*", and that Rorty's pragmatism "is actually the last gasp of this disease" (Rockwell 2004: 143) – but we shall concentrate on his brief discussion of the Putnam–Rorty debate.

Rockwell considers the debate to be mainly over the issue of realism, where Rorty was willing, eager even, to terminate discussion of this issue and move on to something more fruitful whereas Putnam thinks that the first terminating step here is grossly mistaken and that Rorty's arguments for urging it are woefully inadequate. Rockwell interprets Putnam as believing he has overdetermining grounds for saying these are inadequate. First, they fail to take into account the fact that certain metaphysical and epistemological questions, para-digmatically those associated with realism, are unavoidable. And sec-ondly, they embody conceptual incoherencies in any case.

On the first point, Putnam is lining up with some of Rorty's favour-ite targets: philosophers who think that their tradition has identified inescapable problems, the kind that arise naturally as soon as one is able to think and never cease to be troublesome as along as one con-tinues to be able to think (except on those rare occasions that they get solved and this becomes public knowledge or, even rarer, one solves them oneself). Rorty simply would not buy this, and for persuasive reasons. As early as *Philosophy and the Mirror of Nature* (i.e. 1979), he argued that far from arising out of metaphysical thin air, philosophical problems get a leg-up from assumptions that are historically deter-mined. Take away the circumstances that shore up the assumptions and the problem itself is liable to collapse. Interestingly, as well as claiming that the classic pragmatists found metaphysics to be indis-pensable, Rockwell says that they felt the same about philosophical illusions, that "human life requires us to accept some sort of philo-sophical 'illusion'" (2004: 144). And, he cites Putnam's concurrence: "the illusions that philosophy spins are illusions that belong to the nature of human life itself" (*ibid*.). Rorty did not buy this either:

> I do not see how Putnam could tell whether, for example the distinction between 'our experience' and 'the external world', or what Davidson calls the 'scheme-content distinction', is among "the illusions that belong to the nature of human life itself" or is as ephemeral as the distinction between the superlunary quin-tessence and the four sublunary elements has proved to be … The *nature* of human life? Everywhere and always? For all ages to come? Surely not. (1998b: 46)

As for the alleged 'conceptual incoherencies', there is some dif-ficulty in making such a charge stick to someone like Rorty, who is sceptical, if only on Quinean grounds, about the notion of some-thing being conceptually connected with, or necessary for, something else. Quine is famous for repudiating the analytic–synthetic distinc-tion (Quine 1953a), as between truths that hold on account of the meaning of the words used to express them and those that hold on the basis of an associated factual element, the former being necessary and the later contingent. When that distinction goes, the idea of connections that are purely conceptual is undermined. Besides, Rorty showed many times, in the face of such charges, that his claims seemed to lack coherence only to those who refused to take them at face value, who could not resist reading *their own metaphysical assumptions* into them. Consider Putnam's objection, endorsed by Rockwell, that Rorty contradicts himself in "saying that we should reject traditional realism because it is a bad theory, even though the majority of people currently believe it" (2004: 143). For, "what can 'bad' possibly mean here but 'based on the wrong metaphysical picture'" (*ibid.*). To this Rorty replies:

> I quite agree that the relativist cannot [speak of *right* or *wrong* metaphysical pictures] and that I cannot either. But why should either I, or this patsy called 'the Relativist', explicate 'bad' in terms of metaphysical pictures? There are all sorts of occasions on which we can say that our concept of X needs to be changed and old intuitions thrown overboard, not for metaphysical reasons, but for reasons that are called, depending on context, 'ethical' or 'practical' or 'political'. (1998b: 56)

Forster: pragmatism without limit

In his paper "What is at Stake Between Putnam and Rorty?" ([1992] 2004), Paul Forster defends Rorty against Putnam's charge of relativism. He argues that Putnam makes this charge on false pretences because he has misunderstood Rorty's ethnocentrism. He points out that when Putnam observed "We do not have notions of the 'existence' of things or the 'truth' of statements that are independent of the versions we construct and the procedures and practices that give sense to talk of 'existence' and 'truth' within those versions" (1983: 230), he was building bridges (since "this is all that Rorty's ethnocentrism involves"; Forster [1992] 2004: 161). He contends that Rorty was only trying to establish, and only committed to, a "purely negative point that we should drop the traditional distinction between correspondence to reality and view truth as a commendatory term for well justified beliefs" (Rorty 1984: 6). Thus he should not be saddled with a substantive theory of truth. Forster concludes: "Rather than an avowal of relativism, 'ethnocentrism' simply acknowledges the perspectival aspects of inquiry central to Putnam's own pragmatic realism" ([1992] 2004: 161).

Forster's paper was first published in 1992 and is therefore now well behind the times with regard to the whole Putnam–Rorty debate. Nevertheless, his defence of Rorty's ethnocentrism is illuminating, as are his points about the inadequacies of Putnam's transcultural, limit theory of truth as expressed in statements like this one:

> Is there a *true* conception of rationality, a *true* morality, even if all we ever have are our conceptions of these? The very fact that we speak of our different conceptions as different conceptions of *rationality* posits a *Grensbegriff*, a limit-concept of the ideal truth. (Putnam 1981: 216)

Forster comments that appealing to idealized epistemic conditions "seems symptomatic of a vain hope for an ultimate legitimation of our practices" ([1992] 2004: 163). And he acknowledges that for Rorty the positing of 'limit-concept' is yet another attempt to get external validation of our social practices, the kind that cannot be based on anything seen from the inside:

> What is such a posit supposed to do except to say that from God's point of view the human race is heading in the right direction? Surely Putnam's 'internalism' should forbid him to say anything like that. Positing *Grensbegriff* seems merely a way of telling ourselves that a non-existent God would, if he did, exist be pleased with us. (Rorty 1984: 10)

Forster concludes by reminding us that Rorty's ethnocentrism was born out of a rejection of any transcendental viewpoint from which any ultimate grounding of our practices could be derived. It was not intended to stand in for such a viewpoint. Indeed, it can only do its work by keeping a close eye on how things look at ground level:

Rorty is not suggesting that cultural standards are ultimate epistemic principles, rather he is denying that the regress of justification can be halted in this way at all! ... Neither form nor content, mind nor world, serves as an independent variable to which the products of inquiry can be reduced. Nothing about this view precludes the critical (re)assessment of beliefs and standards. The pragmatist need only insist that critical conversation proceeds by comparing the practical advantages of various alternatives under consideration. Such debate can only take place against a backdrop of more or less widely shared beliefs, habits and interests which are themselves defensible only in terms of more beliefs, habits and interests (and by further comparisons with alternatives)   ([1992] 2004: 169)

Conant: Is metaphysics still pulling Rorty's strings?

Metaphysics frequently appears disguised as the rejection of metaphysics.   (Hilary Putnam, *Words and Life*)

In his thoughtful editorial introduction to Putnam's *Words and Life* (1995b), James Conant argues that Putnam has modified his position in ways that entail that he no longer stands by all the views expressed in the five passages cited by Rorty as evidence of substantial areas of agreement. However, what Conant pinpoints as the most important upshot of this is that Putnam has distanced himself from one of Rorty's main reasons for rejecting metaphysical realism. Moreover, Conant seems to think that, in doing so, Putnam has left Rorty in the metaphysical lurch, still trapped by the very picture he wished to erase.

Rorty often characterized his philosophical approach as anti-representationalist. By this he meant that he rejected any notion of representations as philosophical intermediaries, as things that come between us and our world and by means of which we can explicate our significant relationships to that world. Hence he preferred to talk about language in terms of its general utility rather than as a medium of representation. Davidson's philosophy attracted him greatly for this very reason. He saw Davidson as perhaps providing us with the best post-Wittgensteinian ways of discussing language philosophically without appealing to bogus intermediaries.

However, Conant argues that while Putnam and Rorty used to share a view as to how best to show that the metaphysical realism underlying appeals to philosophical intermediaries is highly suspect, Putnam has now moved on. He thinks that view is hostage to what it professes to reject. The view is that since we cannot get out from behind language in order to compare it to the world as it is (i.e. independent of our linguistic conceptions of it), we must conclude that language cannot be a medium of representation – for we can never show *how* it actually works in that respect (because we can never *see* it at work, we can never, as John McDowell puts it, look at language sideways on), and we can never verify that it *is working* (because we cannot make the requisite comparisons). In short, saying language is representational is an empty explanatory gesture.

Putnam suggests that Rorty was wrong to make the impossibility of doing something, such as standing outside our thought and language in order to make comparisons with the world, a reason for rejecting the idea that language can be used to represent things. Rorty made this mistake because he did not reflect carefully enough on the nature and implications of the 'impossibility' he wished to invoke. If he had been more careful, then he would have realized, as Putnam has come to, that the unintelligibility of the task that is supposedly ruled out on grounds of impossibility infects the conclusion that representationalism should be rejected:

> I think the trouble ... comes when one does not properly explore the sort of 'impossibility' which is at issue when one concludes – with Rorty – that such a guarantee [i.e. that the world is such and such independently of our linguistic representation to the effect that it is such and such] is indeed impossible. What I want to emphasize is that Rorty moves from a conclusion about the unintelligibility of metaphysical realism (we cannot have a guarantee – of the sort that doesn't even make sense – that our words represent things outside themselves) to scepticism about the possibility of representation *tout court*. We are left with the conclusion that there is no metaphysically innocent way to say that our words *do* 'represent things outside themselves.' Failing to

93

inquire into the unintelligibility which vitiates metaphysical realism, Rorty remains blind to the way in which his own rejection of
metaphysical realism partakes of the same unintelligibility. The
way in which scepticism is the flip side of a craving for an unintel-
ligible kind of certainty (a senseless craving, one might say, but for
call that a deeply human craving) has rarely been more sharply
illustrated than by Rorty's complacent willingness to give up on
the (platitudinous) idea that language can be used to represent
something outside language. (Putnam 1995b: 231–2)

Conant appears to accept that Rorty argued in the way Putnam
describes here, that he subscribed to the bizarre conclusion that
there is no sense in which language can be reasonably said to represent things outside itself, that he was subject to the strange craving
Putnam alludes to, and that he lost touch with the functions of ordinary words – to the extent that he was unable to retrieve "the humble uses of these words" (in Putnam 1995b: xxvii). But when Rorty
is read with more sensitivity, it is difficult to make any of this stick.
Rorty stated clearly on many occasions that he was perfectly happy
with ordinary words put to humble uses (how, after all, could someone who was so sceptical about the power of philosophy, dismiss
such words, and those uses, on *philosophical* grounds?). His objection was to the representational mystification of those words, the
kind that occurs when philosophers start to make a big deal about
the nature of their relationship to things in the world. Indeed, Conant
acknowledges at one point that Rorty both counselled and practised
'speaking with the vulgar'. However, he does not take into account
the fact that this meant that Rorty did not need to go in for 'retrieval'.
Metaphysically innocent representational uses of words were close at
hand, and he was happy to use them along with everyone else. Thus
it was puzzling to him why some of his critics would cite such uses in
evidence against him, as if their very existence constituted a refuta-
tion of his views.[4] Like James, he regarded the ideas associated with
referring to or corresponding to independent reality as banal when
they were expressed in *ordinary* contexts, the very contexts in which
the relevant words evolved. It was only when philosophers whipped
up a theory behind the backs of such normal linguistic settings,
theories that provoked more problems than they solved, that he

found things to complain about. In his eyes, the shoes of unintelligibility and metaphysical craving were on other feet – in this case Putnam's (and presumably Conant's). We can therefore regard his 'stand outside language' requirement as a typical pragmatist move. Opponents wish to explain the function of language and its relation (and, by extension, the mind's relation) to the world in terms of representations. A pragmatist must ask: what can we *do* with this, practically speaking; what difference does it make? Exploring this further, a pragmatist is likely to find little room for practical manoeuvre. And, in this vein we can think of Rorty saying: 'Look you can only talk this through *within* language. There is nowhere else to go. We cannot set up an experiment to check the representational hypothesis, *as a philosophical hypothesis*, because there is no vantage point from which to check the results.' But, in speaking like this, as he did, he did not cast aspersions on ordinary uses of words to talk about something other than words. Rorty was not indulging the metaphysical sin of taking a certain sort of incoherent craving too seriously, still less, as Putnam rather offhandedly claims, was his attitude towards it indicative of a similar craving in himself ("Why is Rorty so bothered by the lack of a *guarantee* that our words represent things outside themselves? Evidently, Rorty's craving for such a guarantee is so strong that, finding it to be impossible, he feels forced to conclude that our words do not represent anything"; Putnam 1995b: 228). He simply cited the 'impossible task' as a way of highlighting the difficulty in doing anything practically useful with the philosophical notion of representation. He never for one moment intended to deny that ordinary conceptions of that kind are perfectly acceptable and best earn their keep without any interference from philosophy.

Coda: getting to the point

Many of those who have announced the end of the quest for the hidden standard-setting reality have merely continued it under other names.   (Roberto Unger, *The Self Awakened*)

What is the point of all this? We have discovered that Putnam no longer holds a limit theory of truth. And, he no longer subscribes to all the views in the five passages Rorty identified as specifying areas of agreement between the two of them. But then, the purpose of this discussion has not been to finalize the terms of the Putnam–Rorty debate. That would be difficult in any case, not least because Putnam's views are constantly shifting. The aim was rather to show two things. First, we wanted to demonstrate how the New Pragmatism is able to manifest the epistemic virtues of advancing by way of vigorous internal criticism and the trying out of fresh ideas within the context of such criticism. In this sense it clearly practises what it preaches: at no point does the Putnam–Rorty debate, or the commentary on it, deteriorate into mere point-scoring or, still worse, the sort of sloppy uncritical thinking that many critics assume would be rampant if the New Pragmatism were to prevail as a predominant intellectual position. At the same time, the nature of the debate indicates that the New Pragmatism can tolerate a plurality of views without collapsing into vapid mush on that score. The longer the debate continued, the clearer it became that complete reconciliation between the views of Putnam and Rorty is not necessary for the health of the New Pragmatism. Indeed, quite the opposite is true: the sparks caused by the friction between the two thinkers in question generated new ideas and fresh perspectives for the New Pragmatism to thrive on.

The second point was to show that some New Pragmatists, and here Putnam is surely the most important and interesting case, make the best progress in their work by, as it were, thinking *against* their better New Pragmatist selves, and do so by deploying the weapons of traditional enemies. It is not that Putnam is always hammering on the door to escape from his pragmatist prison, but rather that he wants to test it and improve it by trying it out against and, where possible absorbing, more conventional philosophical material from the outside. This probably accounts for the way in which he keeps constantly on the philosophical move. Rorty, by contrast, always seemed to be saying, "It's pretty good in here. Come and take a look." The New Pragmatism can profit greatly from both viewpoints. But, its exponents need to move beyond the Putnam–Rorty debate in order to ignite philosophical themes that no longer hark back to the analytic tradition. By finding ways of talking about human beings and their place in the world that do not invite age-old questions pertinent to those concerns, New Pragmatists can demonstrate that such questions do not arise naturally out of reflection on inherent features of the human condition. They need to walk further along the path that the debate has cleared for them so that they can inhabit the kind of "new philosophical world" envisaged by Rorty:

> In this new world, we shall no longer think of either thought or language as containing representations of reality. We shall be freed both from the subject–object problematic that has dominated philosophy since Descartes and from the appearance–reality problematic that has been with us since the Greeks. We shall no longer be tempted to practice either epistemology or ontology. (2007: 133)

Finally, it is perhaps worth reflecting on Joseph Margolis's assessment of the longer-term outcome of the Putnam–Rorty debate:

> It revivified pragmatism in a most extraordinary way; not gratuitously, it seems, but certainly unexpectedly. The only explanation for its new-found appeal and strength, suddenly perceived even after the exhaustion of the exchange between Rorty and Putnam, must lie in the counterpart admission of the dubious achievements of late analytic philosophy approaching the end of the century: that is in the perceived inadequacies in the work of figures like W. V. Quine and Donald Davidson. So that the quarrel, otherwise a minor affair, actually persuaded the academy of the reasonableness of claims like the following: (a) the basic resources and orientation of classic pragmatism were distinctly promising when compared with the salient forms of scientism favoured by the analysts; (b) pragmatism might well be strengthened by confronting in its own voice the best strategies of analytic philosophy and its deepest questions; (c) pragmatism was in an excellent position to address, perhaps even resolve, the standing differences between Anglo-American and continental philosophy in ways that the analysts could never match; and (d) pragmatism's particular promise lay in its post-Kantian and Hegelian sympathies and intuitions, enhanced by Darwinian proclivities, despite of its not being cast in precisely those terms.

Given the doldrums of Western philosophy at the turn of the century, it looks as if the now minor skirmish between Rorty and Putnam served as a splendid catalyst for the new age. Certainly, it ushers in an entirely new source and prospect of development. (2009: 5)

This provides an interesting backcloth against the discussion of the New Pragmatism's prospects, to which we now turn.

6

PROSPECTS

If there is anything distinctive about pragmatism, it is that it substitutes the notion of a better human future for the notions of 'reality', 'reason', and 'nature'. One may say of pragmatism what Novalis said of Romanticism, that it is the apotheosis of the future. (Richard Rorty, *Philosophy and Social Hope*)

The revival of pragmatism can itself be explained on pragmatic grounds. (Alan Wolfe, *The Missing Pragmatic Revival in American Social Science*)

One of the obstacles to the New Pragmatism's progress in the short term is the resistance of the analytic establishment. Some of this is self-serving.[1] It pays to keep old philosophical disputes going. New Pragmatists deny a selfless version of this. Precisely because there is no *real* pay-off and because they are bored by the lack of genuinely productive results, the 'doldrums' Margolis referred to, they want to stake out uncharted territory, to visit Rorty's promised land where controversies over distinctions such as those between mind and body or appearance and reality seem beside the point and the theories developed to deal with such controversies appear to be irrelevant. There is also a strong element of proper philosophical motivation in the analytic resistance. But even this leaves much to be desired.

A good deal of the intransigence mirrors the reaction of the early critics of classic pragmatism. The old view that social criteria of rationality and truth lead inexorably to relativism on the practical front and self-defeat on the intellectual front is recycled again and again when analytic philosophers confront the New Pragmatism. And the same faults that were displayed by those early critics are compounded in the process: failure to read the relevant texts carefully or with any reasonable degree of intellectual charity; inability to listen to alternative ways of posing the issues at stake; refusal to accept the historical conditionality of philosophical problems; hastiness in reaching for rhetorical guns;[2] zealousness in defence of one's own philosophical turf; sheer nit-picking; and so on. The New Pragmatism's' founding figures showed a good deal of patience when faced with this kind of intransigence. More recent practitioners tend to be less sanguine. This is because, thanks largely to Putnam and Rorty, they are more aware as to how a particular notion, say that of mind, "and the vocabulary in which it is embedded, well illustrates how philosophical analysis and 'intuition', providing mutual support and reinforcement, can entrench a particular set of problems and make them appear mandatory" (Ramberg 2009: 216). Instead of getting caught up in complex debates, the grounding terms of which they dispute, they are more liable to say: why not try doing things this way so that the things you find so problematic are no longer of great concern?

The question as to how the New Pragmatism will fare over the longer term is one that will be answered by the results of experiments in 'doing things differently' and hence by history as it unfolds. But, it is clear now that the New Pragmatism has the best chance of flourishing if it makes further progress outside philosophy. Here, trading on its capacity for innovation, its political flexibility and its autonomous, cosmopolitan and neoteric features, it has a head start. Indeed, it has already begun to exert a strong influence in a number of areas.[3]

In brief, the issue of 'future prospects' will be settled pragmatically. If the New Pragmatism proves to be sufficiently useful beyond the realms of philosophy, it will be able to fulfil more of the potential described in this book. Setting aside, for the moment, the further question as to whether, given the intransigence we have referred to, success *within* philosophy is likely and, even if so, *sufficient,* let us take a look at how the New Pragmatism has exerted influence in the wider sense. The common factor in most cases, other than the key role played by Rorty, is that not only has the New Pragmatism delivered important intellectual results, but it has generated innovative joint ventures, opened up new areas of enquiry and diverted more resources towards them by closing off, or simply ignoring, older, less fruitful areas. There is a wealth of such examples ranging from architecture to music.[4] However, six areas are typical in the sense that either the New Pragmatism has been especially successful therein and we can reasonably expect further profitable advancements, or it is poised to achieve notable results and raise similar expectations: literature, law, feminism, education, politics and religion.[5] We shall consider each of these in turn. There is not enough space to cover any of them in great detail, but we should be able to scratch the surface deeply enough to reveal the great promise of some of the developments that are taking place.

Literature

Art is more moral than moralities.
(John Dewey, *Experience and Nature*)

Philosophers are after all like poets.
(William James, *Pragmatism and The Meaning of Truth*)

Despite its being a kind of magic, [fiction] is actually the enemy of superstition, the slayer of religions, the scrutineer of falsity.
(James Wood, *How Fiction Works*)

The predominant force behind the New Pragmatism's influence on literature was Rorty. His writings helped to dramatically revise the nature of the relationship between literature and philosophy, to the great benefit of both parties.[6] They changed the ways in which literature is viewed and studied. One of the more important effects of this has been to give literature a new cognitive lease of life; it now sits comfortably alongside more orthodox sources of knowledge about human life. Furthermore, this rejuvenation feeds back into philosophy, revitalizing it also in the process.

Although literature produced some of the greatest treasures of Western culture, it seemed to experience a crisis of self-confidence in the face of the achievements of science. Compared to the deep and all-embracing truths about the world that the predicative theories of science yielded, the offerings of novelists and poets appeared to be arbitrary and unreliable: the ephemeral products of imaginations that lacked an anchor to reality. The literary tradition responded to this in various ways. Some writers simply accepted the ascendancy of science and were resigned to preparing no more than garnish for the intellect, leaving scientists to provide its main meals. Others retreated into technical experimentalism and made no attempt to compete with science. Here, there were some successes – we might think of 'magical realism' in the hands of skilled exponents such as Gabriel García Márquez and Salman Rushdie – but those who dealt with science simply by avoiding its forensic gaze could only climb to the precarious heights of celebrity status; they were never going tower over culture in the ways that Wordsworth, Tolstoy and Dostoyevsky did. Or so it seemed.

Some of those who studied literature professionally were less acquiescent. They reacted to this apparent diminishment of their subject matter by upping its own theoretical ante. And they were helped by an influx of exotic theorists in search of a target for their specialized activities. This story is too complex to rehearse here. But, those who want to follow it up will find, via any decent book on modern literary theory, that it starts roughly with the structuralists and ends, although only for the time being, with the deconstructionists. It matters little for our purposes that there were tensions and incompatibilities between the various approaches that tried to lend theoretical credibility to the study of literature. The point to stress is that they provided the requisite jargon, with at least the semblance of a corresponding theoretical apparatus, to allow those involved in literary studies to lay claim to their own brand of rigour and sophistication, the kind that enabled them to at least imagine they could hold their heads up high, or even higher, in the company of scientists.[7] There was, however, another anomaly in this 'theoretical turn' that we cannot overlook here: it upgraded the intellectual ranking of literature at the heavy price of threatening to destroy it. For under theoretical scrutiny, novels and poems lost their magical power: their power to charm, to shock, to seduce and, ultimately to transform. Fortunately, the stage was set for Rorty, a principal architect of the New Pragmatism, to intervene.[8]

He was ideally suited for the task. For years on end he had been castigating philosophers for still succumbing to "the dogma that only where there is correspondence to reality is there the possibility of rational agreement in a special sense of 'rational' of which science is a paradigm" (PMN: 333). Furthermore, he had shown that it is possible to keep the notion of 'objectivity' going in a respectable manner after this dogma is rejected (for instance, by means of intersubjective agreement among experts in the relevant field). Not only that, but Rorty had elevated the role of the imagination and valorized his own version of Harold Bloom's notion of 'the strong poet', "the maker of new words, the shaper of new languages, ... the vanguard of the species" (CIS: 41). Those artists who used their powers of linguistic creation to fashion new self images and explore fresh social possibilities owed no deference to theorists who insisted on trading in the currency of correspondence. They did not need to print their own theoretical currency.

Rorty's writings on literature, and on the relationship between literature and philosophy, have had complex consequences, many of which are still playing themselves out. But, they can be broadly summarized as follows. By arguing, although more explicitly and more emphatically, Dewey's point that scientific discourse is just one among many possible discourses, and by showing more clearly that there is no natural order of priority of discourses, Rorty helped to revitalize literature's self-image and increase its self-esteem. And by getting theory off its back, so that literature could again be read "in search of excitement and hope" (1998b: 137), Rorty enhanced these results. Finally, by praising "the inspirational value of great works of literature",[9] works that "make people think there is more to this life than they ever imagined" (*ibid.*: 133), Rorty reopened an avenue for transforming the self and society.[10] For he reminded us that poems and novels can have the same effect on us as charismatic people: that they can sweep us off our feet, and radically change our view of ourselves and everything else. Furthermore, they can serve a social purpose beyond that of private infatuation and self-creation by increasing tolerance and helping inculcate moral values. A well-written novel that sympathetically portrays people who tend to be marginalized by society on account of prejudice is likely to do more to change social attitudes towards such people than some abstract theoretical argument regarding their right to be treated respectfully.

Under Rorty's impetus, the New Pragmatism has given literature a boost, but it has also done the same for philosophy. Historically, the relationship between philosophy and literature got off to a bad start when Plato wanted to kick poets out of the ideal republic because they were dissemblers, and therefore incapable of paying proper epistemic attention to the true nature of reality.[11] From then on, things did not get much better. Occasionally, certain writers attained the kind of lofty status that enabled them to appropriate the name of philosophy for their art without much complaint – and here one might think of Shelley, for example, who constantly referred to the philosophical virtues of poetry and great poets – but generally the relationship was strained, with philosophy presuming to have the upper intellectual hand. When links were made, they were insubstantial and usually one-sided. Philosophical themes were detected in works of literature, but they were supposedly dealt there with in the sort of amateurish fashion that enabled philosophers to self-contentedly observe: "See how we handle the issues at stake here in a much clearer, more concise, more objective, and professional manner?" By emphasizing the philosophical utility of literature, however, Rorty did not try to reverse the priorities here. He was not interested in showing that, despite received opinion, literature occupied the superior position. He had no time for the idea of superiority in its own right, and saw it as always relative to purposes and situations. Moreover, his approach enabled him to revitalize philosophy in much the same way as literature, and for much the same reasons. He described how philosophy could be liberated from stale theorizing and dead-end problems, reinvigorated the philosophical imagination in the process, and added metaphor, redescription and self-conscious writerly skills to philosophy's repertoire. The upshot was the end of direct competition between philosophy and literature and the start of a period of fertile cooperation that is now well underway. As its chief instigator in Rorty's wake, the New Pragmatism also stands to benefit from the successful outcomes of such cooperation.

Law

As our presidents, political parties, and legislators become even more corrupt and frivolous, we turn to the judiciary as the only political institution for which we can still fell something like awe. This awe is not reverence for the Euclid-like immutability of law. It is the respect for the ability of decent men and women to sit down around tables, argue things out, and arrive at a reasonable consensus.   (Richard Rorty, *Philosophy and Social Hope*)

Legal pragmatism has attracted much attention over the past twenty-five years or so. What is it? And, how is it connected with the New Pragmatism?

Legal pragmatism holds that pragmatic considerations, rather than unalterable principles, form the basis for both the authority of the law and its application via legal judgments. The classic pragmatists clearly had a strong influence on this view. But more recently the New Pragmatism has stimulated further debate and thereby enabled legal pragmatists to develop a more sophisticated conception of their position while, at the same time, helping members of the legal profession itself get a clearer view of what is at stake between those who advocate a pragmatist approach to legal matters and those who oppose it.

Although he did not put nearly as much effort into making an impact on legal concerns as he did in the case of literature, Rorty was still a key player in the developments we have just described. From *Philosophy and the Mirror of Nature* onwards, Rorty's writings created an intellectual ethos within which it became natural for various intellectuals and professional practitioners outside philosophy to try on pragmatist ideas for size, even if only at the prompting of thoughts such as: pragmatism is creating such a stir, maybe we should check and see whether there is anything to it. In the case of the legal profession and those academically concerned with it, classic pragmatism had already made inroads, as we just indicated, so Rorty's writings tended to play somewhat different roles. To those who already had pragmatist leanings, they represented an opportunity to reflect on those tendencies, to see how they stood up under the light of a more recent formulation of pragmatism. And, for those implacably opposed to the pragmatism of the past, Rorty's writings offered them the chance to review their objections, to examine whether they still held water.

David Luban (1998: 275–6) has instructively outlined the key features of legal pragmatism as follows:

- It is eclectic. "The pragmatist mistrusts the pretensions of totalising Big Think theories to capture all that is important in law. The pragmatist is willing to give every theory a hearing, however, and to appropriate insights from any source if they seem useful."
- It is results orientated or instrumental. "Its focus is on the well-being of the community, not the purity or integrity of legal doctrine. Pragmatists nevertheless recognise that conforming to inherited legal doctrine and attending to history may be good for the community, so doctrinal integrity remains instrumentally important."
- It is history conscious. "Pursuing the good for *this* community requires us to know and respect its unique history. Thus a pragmatist is *historically minded*."
- It is antiformalist. "Formalism is always the enemy of pragmatism. By formalism, I mean cabining legal analysis to logical and analogical manipulation of pre-existing doctrine."

Luban uses this outline to further a complex, ongoing and wide-ranging debate that has been one of the main causes of the greater sophistication we referred to earlier. This is the debate as to whether legal pragmatism has any substantial connection to philosophical pragmatism of any kind, be it 'classic' or 'new'.

Some legal pragmatists, the old guard, as it were, consider their attitude to matters of law to be based, *of necessity*, on the philosophical presuppositions of classic pragmatism. Their critics dispute the necessity invoked here. Luban concedes that if legal pragmatism is defined uncontroversially, as above, in terms of its eclecticism, results orientation, historical consciousness and antiformalism, then it is true that it need have no connection with classic pragmatism. For, as Luban puts it, "you can reach these same four very general features from a wide variety of philosophical perspectives" (*ibid.*: 276).

Moreover, according to Luban, any putative connection with classic pragmatism becomes blurred by controversy when legal pragmatism oversteps the boundaries marked out by these general features, as it needs to do to escape banality, and as it does do, or so he claims, in the hands of one of its most famous exponent, Richard Posner, who defends a number of substantive philosophical positions.[12] Luban seems to see no way out of controversy here until philosophy settles the issues at stake. But, this puts legal pragmatism in a tricky situation. To carry weight it must venture deeper into philosophical territory and yet, as Luban acknowledges, it would be impractical, and probably futile given past performances, for legal pragmatists to sit around waiting for philosophy to make up its mind on contentious matters. As an aside, he applauds what he regards as the 'subtlety' of Thomas Grey's contention "that legal pragmatism requires no philosophical foundations *including foundations in the philosophy that says that legal pragmatism requires no philosophical foundations*" (Luban 1998: 277–8).

However, far from being subtle, this contention betrays a lack of understanding of how the New Pragmatism relates to legal pragmatism. Furthermore, Luban himself manifests a similar lack when he concludes that, in the end, despite the dilemma that the requisite involvement entails, legal pragmatism cannot be philosophically freestanding. It is time to see what happened when Rorty entered the fray.

In response to Luban and other contributors to an interesting mini-version of the overall debate (see Grey 1998; Posner 1998), Rorty clarified how the New Pragmatism is connected with legality in general, and not just legal pragmatism. Although he did not state this outright, he implied that Grey's allegedly 'subtle' contention misses the point of the New Pragmatism. Talk of providing foundations, even paradoxical talk is irrelevant. The New Pragmatism never attempts to provide 'foundations', not even in the attenuated sense of a *non-foundational* basis for something. It relates to things very differently: in virtue of its general utility.

The New Pragmatism is useful to legal pragmatists because it helps them both practise law and come to a reflective understanding of how and why they do so, without carrying unwieldy and potentially distracting philosophical baggage. For Rorty, those who want to embed legal practices in philosophy, those who, like Luban, claim that "arguments central to the law presuppose philosophical positions" (1998: 292), were guilty of subscribing to an outmoded picture of philosophy. This is a depiction in which philosophy's problems are inescapable, "come naturally to the human mind, and arise independently of the mind's socio-historical circumstances" (Rorty 1998d: 308). Against this, Rorty offered a New Pragmatist portrait within which such problems are viewed as optional, and *a fortiori* not indispensable in legal contexts. The New Pragmatism can help legal pragmatism by showing how to steer past patches of philosophical quicksand, and it can best do so by tackling a task that, as Rorty pointed out, was first articulated by Dewey: "the task of future philosophy is to clarify men's ideas as to the social and moral strifes of their day" (RP: 94). But, in carrying out this task, it will need to find creative ways of talking about legal issues that meet the day-by-day requirements of legal practice and do not incite any yearning for philosophical backup.

Feminism

> By bringing feminist insights to pragmatism, pragmatist feminism helps develop the radical potential of American philosophy that was not always fully recognised by its founders.
> (Shannon W. Sullivan, "Feminism")

One of the main reasons some feminists have viewed classic pragmatism as a promising ally, as something that can bring insights to *them*,[13] is that it offers the opportunity to evade the pitfalls of a male-dominated philosophical tradition while itself appearing to be ripe for the introduction of an outlook hitherto ignored, if not actively excluded: one informed by the variegated, knowledge-infused, historically conditioned, experiences of women. Here, for example, is a quotation from Dewey that seems very hospitable to this line:

> Women have as yet made little contribution to philosophy, but when women who are not mere students of other persons' philosophy set out to write it, we cannot conceive that it will

be the same in viewpoint or tenor as that composed from the standpoint of the different masculine experience of things.

(RP: 19)

However, the very difference that Dewey refers to cuts no ice with the New Pragmatism. It prefers to avoid philosophical appeals to experience, even when historically contextualized and as charitably defined as James's and Dewey's holistically inclusive versions. How, then, does the New Pragmatism relate to feminism?

A good start to answering this question can be made by way of considering, yet again, one of Rorty's prolific and provocative interventions. In his article "Feminism and Pragmatism" (1998b: 202–27), Rorty's first substantial public discussion of the topic, he suggests a number of ways in which "Pragmatist philosophy might be useful to feminist politics" (*ibid.*: 206). His advice encompasses typical New Pragmatist strategies for surmounting the obstacles posed by traditional philosophy while also making its own views more socially serviceable.

The New Pragmatism recognized how the progress of classic pragmatism was nipped in the bud by precipitous criticism, the kind that James and Dewey colluded with by taking it too seriously, while unconsciously sharing some of its assumptions. And having also struck out on its own path before philosophical history had a chance to repeat itself, it is well placed to help feminism forge ahead regardless.

As Rorty so frequently reminded us, 'regardless' means dropping superfluous traditional philosophical idioms, those that generate age-old problems that swarm around the appearance–reality distinction and notions of realism, universalism, essences, timeless objectivity and so forth. It also means largely ignoring the criticisms that are bound to be unleashed when this is attempted, criticisms that seek to show that the price of disregarding such problems is far too high, and that anyone who does so is irredeemably reckless. In Rorty's New Pragmatist lexicon, regardlessness of this kind does not equate to loss of objectivity and the abandonment of adequate intellectual standards. It does not lead to relativism. As a pragmatist, Rorty was concerned first and foremost with *practical* integrity and efficacy, and he argued that these qualities can be achieved, indeed, can *best* be achieved, outside the framework of problem-mongering concepts drummed up by the philosophical tradition in the forlorn hope of subordinating social practices to the dictates of theory. He pointed out that much feminist literature can be read as having already heeded some of the lessons of the New Pragmatism and can therefore be interpreted as saying things like:

> We are *not* appealing from phallist appearance to nonphallist reality. We are *not* saying that the voice in which women will some day speak will be better at representing reality than present-day masculist discourse. We are not attempting the impossible task of developing a nonhegmonic discourse, one in which truth is no longer connected with power. We are not trying to do away with social constructs in order to find something that is not a social construct. We are just trying to help women out of the traps that men have constructed for them, help them get the power they do not presently have, and help them create a moral identity as women. (1991b: 210)

If feminism joins forces with the New Pragmatism, then it should find it easier to keep talking more and more like this rather than backsliding into old-time philosophy speak. However, Rorty was careful to acknowledge that in this regard, the benefits that feminism can enjoy are modest. He did not profess modesty out of fear of being thought of as just one more condescending male thinker trying to tell women what to do and how to run their lives. His modesty was impersonal. It concerned the limitations of philosophical power.

Philosophical movements tend to be insignificant compared to social movements. And, since the New Pragmatism does not try to provide intellectual grounding for anything ("we are not in the foundations business"; *ibid.*: 212), all it can do is help keep feminism out of philosophical trouble, and offer "a few pieces of special-purpose ammunition – for example, some additional replies to charges that their aims are unnatural, their demands irrational, or their claims hyperbolic" (*ibid.*).

There is, however, a second, more exciting and more ambitious New Pragmatist theme that Rorty developed alongside this special-purpose ammunition. Feminism has made much progress by redescribing the past in ways that do two important things. First, the balance between the respective cultural contributions of men and women is realigned in terms that are more favourable to women. This is done by allowing voices to be heard that were originally suppressed or ignored. A telling example involves the contribution that women made to classic pragmatism. It has been made much clearer, for instance, that Jane Addams was "responsible for the conception of democracy as not just a political system, but as a way of life, which became the centrepiece of Dewey's pragmatism" (Sullivan 2009, alluding to Seigfried 2002: xi). The second achievement has been to highlight the deprivation, humiliation and suffering that women have been subjected to on account of their enforced subservience to males. Rorty did not deny the importance of these projects. However, he argued that feminism can, and should, do more than set the historical record straight and clear away male-constructed obstacles in order to further its aim of making life better for women now and in the future. It would be selling such lives short if feminism's main goals were only adequate recognition for the past achievements of women, acknowledgment of how they were wronged and removal of the barriers placed in their path by gender-biased, cultural practices. These goals are not sufficiently radical. Furthermore, they assume that women have some kind of mysterious, culture-independent existence: that they have been waiting throughout history, wholly preformed in their own right, to burst out from the shell of oppressive social circumstances and demonstrate their parity with men. Rorty suggested that feminism adopt the New Pragmatism's approach to self-creation, that it spend more time on "helping to create women rather than attempting to describe them more accurately" (1998b: 218).[14] This project is utopian. It offers women the prospect of living their very own lives in the radical sense of lives as yet unlived or even imagined by anyone. So created, women will come to possess new ways of talking about themselves that suit their freshly acquired aims and aspirations; they will have gained, as Rorty nicely put it, "semantic authority over themselves" (*ibid.*: 225).

The New Pragmatism is well suited to help feminists embark on such an ambitious project. For it "allows for the possibility of expanding logical space, and thereby for an appeal to courage and imagination rather than to putatively neutral criteria" (*ibid.*: 228).

And, no one should doubt that the creation of a "new and better sort of human being" (*ibid*.: 227) requires, perhaps more than anything else, courage and imagination.

Education

> If we are willing to conceive education as the process of forming fundamental dispositions, intellectual and emotional, towards nature and fellow men, philosophy may even be defined as the general theory of education.
>
> (John Dewey, *Democracy and Education*)

Dewey prefaced the above remarks with the claim that "the educational point of view enables one to envisage the philosophical problems where they arise, and thrive, where they are at home, and where acceptance or rejection makes a difference in practice" (DE: 31). And, despite the unnerving vagueness that infected his prose (What is "the educational point of view"? What is it that is accepted or rejected?), it is easy to see why it seemed natural for Dewey to make a strong connection between philosophy and education. His views on this connection and on education in general have moved in and out of fashion. They ceased to be as influential when they were somewhat unfairly blamed for the excesses of progressive educational methods, as we mentioned in Chapter 4, and then they remained in the intellectual background after philosophy of education went analytic, using methods of linguistic and so-called conceptual analysis to drain the subject of the sort of interest that Dewey's alternative approach might have inspired. More recently, under the prompting of the Putnams in particular, Dewey's philosophy of education has attracted interest on account of the help it may belatedly provide in dealing with the severe social problems that threaten to undermine the educational systems of the Western democracies. In their paper "Education for Democracy", for example, Hilary and Ruth Anna Putnam show, among other things, how Dewey's educational recommendations clarify these problems by throwing them into relief against the background of an educational regime that now looks as desirable as it does idealistic. After noting that Dewey claimed "the increasing complexity of social life requires a longer period of infancy [in which to acquire the powers needed to deal with those complexities]" (Putnam & Putnam 1995b: 228), the Putnams also note the stark contrast with modern trends:

> On this point our society now seems at odds with itself. We have adopted longer years of schooling as the norm, yet we have allowed infancy to be shortened through earlier sexual activity and earlier involvement with drugs and violence. (*Ibid.*: 228)

Does this mean that classic pragmatism is set for some sort of revival in the field of education? And, where does the New Pragmatism fit into the picture?

While classic pragmatism has always been closely linked with education because of Dewey, regardless of fluctuations in the popularity of his views, the New Pragmatism has generally been dissociated from it because Rorty made such a strong claim to the effect that it should be. In responding to papers by Carol Nicholson (1989) and Rene Arcilla (1990) that suggested his philosophy could have a salutary effect on education, Rorty denied that his philosophy had any useful relevance. Moreover, as Kenneth Wain reminds us, "elsewhere he went even further, describing the intrusion of philosophy into education not just as irrelevant, but as downright harmful, clouding practical issues and rendering them completely intractable" (2001: 163).[15] What are we to make of this? Is education simply a no-go area for the New Pragmatism? Will its prospects for influencing social life be dimmed if classic pragmatism moves in to fill the philosophical vacuum?

Rorty's scepticism about the value of applying philosophy to education was the product of his scepticism about philosophy in general. He did not think that the kinds of issues that philosophers are likely to be concerned about in the field of education are interesting or susceptible to solutions. And, he thought this holds true even of his own pragmatist approach. Is that the end of the story?

It need not be. And, as we shall show, it is not likely to be. Although, Rorty is a key figure within the New Pragmatism, he is not its pope. It is consistent, and probably necessary, for other New Pragmatists to stand towards him as he stood to James and Dewey:

taking him to be a source of inspiration and stimulation rather than doctrinal guidance. Any New Pragmatists worth their salt will know how to tackle a subject like education without invoking dubious philosophical apparatus and without being inclined to see intractable philosophical problems lurking behind issues that simply needed to be ironed out by finding practical compromises among opposing parties. They will, in short, have learned to display the kind of self-effacing, philosophical modesty we described earlier in connection with Rorty's approach to feminism. For the New Pragmatists, there are no forbidden areas, although there may be many that are not worth visiting or will turn out to have been such.

Education is in a mess in most countries, and not just an economic mess. Given that it is connected with virtually every other facet of social life, the New Pragmatist who thinks primarily in terms of furthering the human good, of using philosophy to make a practical difference to people's lives, is bound to be drawn towards education, if only as a challenging and intriguing test case. Besides which there are two good reasons for being so drawn that we have already touched on.

First, there is renewed interest in Dewey's work on education. This interest is most likely to bear fruit if Dewey's position is taken at pragmatist face value rather than as encouragement for a revival of classic pragmatism; that is, if he is interpreted as making concrete practical suggestions for improving educational practices. The New Pragmatists are well equipped to do this. They have no commitments to Dewey's philosophy as such, and no illusions that it might be worth resurrecting wholesale. Indeed, the Putnams have already shown the way. In "Education for Democracy" (1995b), they extract a wealth of interesting practical proposals for addressing modern educational problems from Dewey's *Democracy and Education* and *Experience and Education*. They suggest that Dewey's views have regained relevance because "we stand today at a place very much like that occupied by Dewey in 1938" (*ibid.*: 221). However, they are very careful, in New Pragmatist spirit, to be selective: to focus only on what is likely to be useful in resolving some of the issues facing us *now*.

The second reason why New Pragmatists are liable to find themselves attracted towards the field of education looks, at first blush, a bit paradoxical. For they will take their cue from Rorty. Although Rorty was quite adamant that his contributions to philosophy were not pertinent to matters of education, there are various interesting suggestions scattered throughout his writings that impinge on just such matters. Furthermore, since other New Pragmatists need not abide by Rorty's own strictures and, indeed, may feel entitled to overrule him on his own Pragmatist grounds (e.g. "We find some stuff in Rorty's writings that can be usefully related to educational issues despite his strenuous denials to that effect" or "It seems to us, that there are better ways to interpret his philosophical output than Rorty himself realized, and some of these attribute an educational significance to it"). New Pragmatists will not be moved to try to work Rorty's insights up into anything like a systematic theory of education. But, they may deploy them on an *ad hoc* basis to help defuse hot-headed debates about the nature of course content (Rorty said that early on, the basic skills of the culture need to be taught rather matter-of-factly, and then, as they get older, students should be encouraged to gain inspiration from, and sharpen their critical teeth on, great texts, some of which challenge what they have already been taught – but not too much fuss should be made about which ones). Or, New Pragmatists may make Rortyan moves to bring lofty theoretical debates down to earth, debates about, for example, whether educationalists should try to inculcate the truth, and whether this is possible (here, Rorty claimed it is better to teach students the skills required to achieve informed consensus, while cultivating the mindset that embodies both confidence and fallibilism – confidence in the outcome of such consensus and acceptance that it could turn out to be wrong-headed, that, however compelling it seems, some better informed consensus may come to overturn it). Even Rorty's avowed negativity can be put to good use in combating the theoretical excesses of educationalists.

By turning back to what is salient in Dewey's large body of work on education and by working through the consequences of Rorty's insights, the New Pragmatists may be able to ensure that pragmatism is once again a vital force for the good in educational theory and practice.

Politics

It is unfortunate, I think, that many people hope for a tighter link between philosophy and politics than there is or can be.
(Richard Rorty, *Philosophy and Social Hope*)

I envisage a global utopia in which nobody – neither the philosophers nor the masses – thinks that democratic institutions need any more than pragmatic justification.　　　　(*Ibid.*)

There has been a resurgence of interest in the political significance of pragmatism.[16] Much of this has been stimulated by the New Pragmatism. In asserting its autonomy, in breaking free from the concerns of the tradition that sidetracked James and Dewey, thwarting their larger ambitions in the process, it has encouraged many philosophers, and thinkers from other disciplines, to take a fresh look at classic pragmatism's agenda for social improvement. Given Dewey's emphasis on political affairs, and his passion for democracy in particular, this has naturally led to an intensive reconsideration of his contribution to political theory.

In Chapter 4, we discussed in some detail how Hilary Putnam claims to have retrieved an 'epistemological argument for democracy' from Dewey's work. This attempted retrieval has generated some interesting and ingenious attempts to improve on Putnam's formulation of the argument.[17] But, there have also been other independent New Pragmatist initiatives that manifest more suspicion of the theoretical aspects of both this argument and the reconsideration of Dewey's work in general. Here, once again, Rorty is a key figure.

His view of the relationship between philosophy and politics was very similar to his negative assessment of that between philosophy and education: there is none, and we fall into all sorts of errors when we try to forge one. Nevertheless, he made an important contribution to political debates, wrote much interesting and provocative material about liberalism, mainly in its non-philosophical defence, and opened up new themes for New Pragmatists to explore. So what was going on?

Rorty's negative view, as we have called it, was primarily a cautionary one. He warned against allowing traditional philosophy, with all it flaws and grandiose theoretical illusions, to gain authority over politics.[18] This kind of philosophy is obsessed with truth, or rather 'Truth', viewing it "in the Platonic way" (1991b: 192). So viewed, said Rorty, it "is simply not relevant to democratic politics" (*ibid.*). What such politics requires, instead, are practical proposals as to how to set things up so that people can enjoy the optimum degree of freedom to pursue enquiry and refine their relevant skills accordingly. But, Rorty was not just concerned about protecting political discourse from getting derailed by irrelevancies or falling into theoretical errors, he wanted it to assume its proper pragmatic status whereby political arrangements instil confidence solely on account of their capacity to make an appropriate practical difference to people's lives. His forthright views on political matters constituted a robust retort in the face of what Matthew Festenstein rightly identifies as a key question arising out of the recrudescence of interest in pragmatic conceptions of politics: "Does a doctrine with a professed bias for practice leave room for a theoretical account of politics?" (2001: 203).

Rorty answered the question by dismissing it. But not by *simply* dismissing it. He explained why he thought it was a bad question, why he thought that using theory to ground politics, or giving it priority over politics in any other substantial sense, is a bad idea. And, he repeated his reasons for thinking this in a number of writings. In summary, they amount to this: theory should be downgraded because it has no useful role to play in the defence of democratic institutions and, furthermore, there are more productive ways of thinking and talking about politics.

For Rorty, politics involves arranging social circumstances to create good societies. But, such societies are not to be defined according to neutral criteria that sit up high in the philosophical sky, above the turmoil of political activity, at least some of which is bound to generate conflict. They are defined in terms of their capacity to both encourage and allow people to be good. And here again, the relevant sense of 'goodness' is defined at ground level, and in practical terms. It is not simply *moral* goodness, but something broader, something that cashes out as living a good life, where this, in turn, is fleshed out as an indeterminate mix of individualism and sociability. Individualism comes into the picture via private projects, subsumed at the most general level, by the project of self-creation. And sociability comes in through sensitivity to the plight of others – as when they fail in their most precious personal projects or incur harm in other ways – and the capacity to view increasing numbers and types of people as being just another human being, as being 'one of us'. Rorty called the result of exercising this capacity 'solidarity'. But, we should not think of this as a big love-in or an amorphous merging of spirits. It includes respect for 'otherness', for the space in which to be different and to pursue different projects. Rorty's political utopia is a place in which people have the freedom to pursue multiple projects of self-creation and a sensibility that enables them to applaud and identify with the projects of others, at least to the extent of viewing them as projects that 'people like us' should be allowed to care about. As we describe this utopia, it becomes clear that traditional theoretical discourse has little to do with it. And, sure enough, Rorty invited us to describe, explain and usher in such a utopia by other means: ethnography, journalism, literature (poetry for self-creation and novels for the development of appropriate social sensitivity on top of that), narrative, docudrama and even comic books (CIS: xvi).[19] This pluralistic approach not only replaces that of traditional philosophical theorizing about politics, but also casts aside the high-theoretical posturing of leftists. Rorty held them to be just as guilty as more orthodox philosophers of spinning fantasies about detecting the true nature of an underlying reality that divert attention from the task of helping more and more people organize themselves so as to be able to lead better and better lives.

By gesturing towards a liberal utopia and some general methods for helping create it, Rorty left many questions unanswered: who is to decide what constitutes a social improvement and what does not? How far should the acceptance of tolerance extend, and who gets to decide this? And so forth. His critics will try to turn these against him by taking them to be questions that should be voiced from a neutral vantage point. But, his fellow New Pragmatists are more likely to consider them as more grist for the mill of practical enquiry and thank him for raising them.

Religion

Religion is perhaps the most recent and the most challenging topic to be taken up by New Pragmatists. As such, things are still very much in flux, and it is only possible to give a very brief, rough sketch at this stage as to how things might turn out. Nevertheless, religion is an important topic and even the vague promise of achieving something new and interesting, something that surpasses the reductive, 'yet-another-demonstration-of-the-impossibility-of-proving-the-existence-of-god', rut that the philosophy of religion has been stuck in for decades is newsworthy.

In turning their attention to religion, the New Pragmatists are, of course, following in the footsteps of the classic pragmatists, and those of James in particular. James announced that one of the chief aims of pragmatism was to accommodate religion and yet still "preserve the rich intimacy of the facts" (PMT: 23). But, when he discussed how it would treat "positive religious constructions cordially" (*ibid.*) his position seemed unstable. He veered between the extremes of empiricist reduction (religious constructions are fine as long as they square directly with the facts) and the kind of open-ended criteria of convenience or expediency that Russell and other early opponents of pragmatism found so abhorrent ("On pragmatic principles, if the hypothesis of God works satisfactorily in the widest sense of the word, it is true"; *ibid.*: 143). James's empiricist option continued to be influential as philosophers tried to develop its naturalistic aspects without taking on the burden of reduction.[20] But his sanction of open-ended criteria simply provided further ammunition to critics who claimed that the pragmatist conception of truth was overly licentious. To be fair to James, he attached qualifications to his 'religious-claims-are-true-if-they-work' view. The claims in question cannot simply work in a restricted context, they cannot just work *for me* or for *some of us* in isolation; they need to pass the test of holistic verification:

> If theological ideas prove to have a value for concrete life, they will be true for pragmatism, in the sense of being *good for so much*. For how much more they are true, *will depend entirely on their relations to other truths that also have to be acknowledged.* (*Ibid.*: 40–41, emphasis added)

> Now what ever [religion's] residual difficulties may be, experi-
> ence shows that it certainly does work ... the problem is to build
> it out and determine it so that it will *combine satisfactorily with
> all other working truths.*　　　　　(*Ibid.*: 143, emphasis added)

But to give reasonable credit to his critics, James never did think things through sufficiently. He never examined whether religion would pass the ultimate pragmatist test that he himself devised and set so much store by. So by his own lights, the truth of religion remained indeterminate.

The New Pragmatists turn to James mainly for inspiration on the topic of religion, as they so often do in other cases, but they have lit-tle interest in returning to his task of reconciliation, at least not on his terms. They tend to look at religion afresh, independently of the traditional philosophical agenda. It is almost as if they are thinking, "Here is religion. What, if anything, can we say about it? What can we *do* with it?" And, if they are asking *themselves* these questions, there is someone they can refer and respond to, someone who has already said quite a lot.

Late in his philosophical career, Rorty took a religious turn: not in the sense that he converted to a particular religion, but rather in the sense that he started to devote time to discussing the role of religion in general. It can seem puzzling as to why he should do this. Given his atheistic position, why did he not simply let philosophical talk about religion die out? Why risk extending its lifespan by contribut-ing to conversations about it?

There were two reasons. First, as a pragmatist, Rorty had to face up to real life. And although *philosophical* talk about religion might peter out, religion itself was going be around for a long time. It thus remained something that needed to be dealt with. Furthermore, it represented an interesting and challenging test case for what he called 'cultural politics': the kind of politics that philosophers should prac-tise in order to make "efforts to modify people's sense of who they are, what matters to them, and what is most important" (2007: ix).

By placing issues regarding religion within the domain of cultural politics, Rorty thought he had found a way to put a stop to tradi-tional philosophical talk about it. Questions concerning whether God exists, ontological questions, would give way to more general, socially relevant questions about the efficacy of language that contains reference to God. And empirical questions – 'Can religious claims be substantiated by appealing to facts?' – would suffer a similar fate. Rorty's critics will regard the idea of increasing the jurisdiction of cultural politics in this way with disdain. It seemingly leaves Rorty worse off than James at his worst. In the Darwinian cultural battle for ideas, prejudice, dogmatism, economic and military power, not to mention public relations, will determine outcomes, even as truth goes missing.

New Pragmatists will view things differently. They will be grateful to Rorty for introducing an approach to religious issues that does not keep recycling the questions traditionally raised by such issues. For they will see the futility of waiting on unmediated truth, facts, reality or whatever. What they make of Rorty's contributions to the philosophy of religion should spark off some interesting developments in a field that has long been barren.

Across the continental divide

> No one contributed more to making Heidegger's name more respectable in the Anglo-American world in recent years than Richard Rorty.
> (Charles Guignon & David Hiley, *Richard Rorty*)

The New Pragmatism starts with local standards, be they moral, aesthetic, epistemic or whatever, but it does not have to stop there. It can spread its wings, and likes to do so. 'This is how *we* do things', the slogan of Rorty's ethnocentrism,[21] one that is always short for something like 'This is how we do things around here, and we stand by what we do', makes, however, no imperialistic gestures. It is not underpinned by dogma, but rather always accompanied by an acute awareness of its own fallibility – 'It could turn out that we have made a mistake or that there is a better way of doing things' – that leaves everything open to negotiation. This accounts for the lack of tension between the New Pragmatism's preference for making the best of what is in the vicinity, as it were, and its cosmopolitanism: its fondness for foreign flight.

The capacity to stand firm and yet negotiate has enabled the New Pragmatism to branch out in directions that are often closed off to other philosophical approaches. That is the benefit of its willingness to negotiate. And, it has been able to do so without undermining its own identity. That is the advantage of its ability to stand firm. Its relationship to so-called continental philosophy[22] is a case in point.

Analytic philosophy, still the dominant tradition within most universities and institutions of higher learning in the West, tends to set itself apart from the kind of philosophical thinking that runs from Hegel's work through that of Nietzsche, Heidegger and Foucault to its apotheosis in Derrida's writings.[23] But there is a good deal of hostile pride in this 'setting apart'. Analytic philosophers tend to believe that *only they* have identified the key concerns and methods of philosophy: that their counterparts in the continental tradition are on completely the wrong track in those respects. Indeed, they are likely to baulk at the very mention of 'counterparts' because they dispute that continental thinkers belong in the same league as themselves, as *real* philosophers. Hardliners even maintain everything that has been said within the continental tradition that is worth saying can be said more clearly and to more purpose in analytic terms. The rest is just rhetorical froth, some of which is intellectually poisonous.

New Pragmatist's are very sceptical about the analytic appropriation of philosophy. Not only do analytic philosophers have no exclusive rights to the definition of philosophy, along with its problems and its methods, but the one they actually operate with has a problematic history and, at its most forthright and honest, has often veered towards self-mutilation.

The New Pragmatism's attitude to the continental tradition is flexible and open-minded. It looks on that tradition as a potential source of interesting and exciting ideas. And here Rorty was exemplary. He found profitable material in Hegel with which to further elaborate on the reasons for considering philosophical thought to be historically constituted and for abandoning sterile conceptual divisions in favour of a thoroughgoing holism in which words feed one another meaning and significance. Nietzsche was a source of inspiration on similar historicist grounds, but also for his robust account of self-creation and his capacity to verbally unsettle deep-seated philosophical assumptions, especially those connected with realism. Heidegger was enlisted as a staunch ally in Rorty's deconstruction of Platonic metaphysics, a metaphysics that did not lose influence just because analytic philosophers stopped reading Plato carefully and taking the *Dialogues* and the *Republic* seriously.[24] And, finally, Derrida was taken into the fold as an example of someone who, in his later work at least, had discovered how to philosophize, in a playful and entirely writerly way, outside the constraints of the philosophical obsession with problems and methods on both sides of the great divide.

In *Philosophy and the Mirror of Nature*, Rorty identified a category of philosophers who subvert tradition even as they create new ways of thinking and talking. He called them "peripheral pragmatists", and they can be viewed as prototypical New Pragmatists:

> These peripheral, pragmatic philosophers are skeptical primarily *about systematic philosophy*, about the whole project of universal commensuration. In our time, Dewey, Wittgenstein, and Heidegger are the great edifying, peripheral, thinkers. All three make it as difficult as possible to take their thought as expressing views on traditional philosophical problems, or as making constructive proposals for philosophy as a cooperative and progressive discipline. They make fun of the classic picture of man, the picture which contains systematic philosophy, the search for universal commensuration in a final vocabulary. They hammer away at the point that words take their meaning from other words rather than by their representative character, and the corollary that vocabularies acquire their privileges from the men who use them rather than their transparency to the real.
>
> (PMN: 368)

New Pragmatists are able to span traditions precisely because they are 'peripheral': they stand outside traditions other than the one they themselves are forging. This leaves them open to the charge of standing nowhere. But they shrug this off by pointing out that their eclecticism, their tendency to take from *anywhere* whatever they can make use of in furthering the contingent projects that interest them, is a sign of strength, of a certain kind of firm footing, and that it is the dogmatists of tradition, unconsciously immersed in spurious philosophical assumptions, who have planted their feet in quicksand.

However, New Pragmatists are often more peripheral than their prototypes. Rorty showed why. His argument that a viable form of pragmatism needed to liberate itself from its own past extended even to those who were bold enough to indicate a way forward, and applied on *both* sides of the continental divide. Hence, Rorty not only pointed out that on the analytic side Quine, for example, lacked the courage of his pragmatist convictions, a failing that he also believed Davidson also displayed in the end, but he found analogous short-comings in key continental thinkers including, perhaps most impor-tantly, Heidegger and, perhaps most surprisingly, Derrida.

Peripheral thinkers are good at debunking the grand pretensions of their predecessors, but they really excel when they break new ground by, for instance, introducing new big words to get obsessed about. Rorty's general attitude to the continental tradition was that it became fixated on words such as 'power', 'nihilism' and 'alterity' in ways that rendered them as stale and yet problematic as the big bad words of the analytic tradition: they became things that nothing much could be done with outside the academy. In Heidegger's case, a once-promising vocabulary that was built up initially around the term 'Being' and took a contemplative-poetic turn in his later writings (see Pattison 2000) began to look as if the words it contained – words such as 'releasement' (as in 'releasement to things' or 'releasement to the mystery') and 'Dwelling' – had assumed a privileged status because they put humans in touch with something more profound than themselves, something deeper than their social practices. This was the kind of status that Rorty wanted to deny to *any* words. As for Derrida, he exposed the futility of the kind of word-mystification that Heidegger still practised despite all his solemnity regarding similar failings in others. For he showed it up for what it was: metaphysics in one of its most insidiously beguiling forms. Then Derrida began, playfully, sometimes ironically, sometimes in jest, to let words be just what they are: contingent signs with multiple connotations, capable of serving multiple purposes. But Derrida never convinced Rorty that he believed he *was* doing just that and believed it was enough for him to be doing *just* that. In Rorty's eyes, Derrida wavered; he wanted to do better, philosophically speaking, to achieve something more seri-ous, and so he could not resist letting metaphysics have its last gasp even in the midst of his displays of linguistic virtuosity against it. In

Derrida's hands, some words also became too big for their beauti-ful, ingeniously crafted, philosophical boots. Drawing a line through some of them did nothing to change the situation.[25] And here, in the end, Rorty sees an invidious contrast with Wittgenstein:

> We read Wittgenstein as a therapeutic philosopher, whose importance lies in helping us escape from ways of using words that generate pseudo problems. But, for all the jokey and raun-chy desublimizing that goes on in Derrida's books, it is not clear that such an escape, escape from a dusty fly bottle, is what he wants. (1998b: 332)

The New Pragmatists are, as we said, open minded about the con-tinental tradition. This means that, unlike many members of the ana-lytic tradition, they do not write it off. But, there are constraints. The kinds of criticisms of Heidegger and Derrida that Rorty voiced, criti-cisms that provoked reactions almost as hostile as those emanating from the analytic camp, are liable to impress them. For, like Rorty, they want to keep language alive so that it can be used to achieve things, to facilitate personal and social goals. They do not want it to be tied up for too long in metaphysical knots around some idi-osyncratic words that certain thinkers get philosophically hung up on. There is, in the New Pragmatist attitude, the feeling that being is best kept light, best left undarkened by the mirage of deeper des-tiny conjured up by thinkers who fear the idea of a culture built on self-reliance, social confidence and solidarity instead of something far greater, something beyond the merely human. But, many conti-nental thinkers find this attitude disturbing. They seem to associate the lightness that comes from untethering thought from philosoph-ical ontology and tying it to social purposes with superficiality, with a crass insensitivity to the great mystery and pathos of the human condition. This means that they are inclined to defend their most precious words of thought fiercely, to hang on to them just as tightly as analytic philosophers hang on to such words as 'truth', 'reason', 'reality' and 'objectivity'. There is also 'hostile pride' on this side of the 'divide'. But, it should not prevent New Pragmatists from scaveng-ing for ideas even as they try to negotiate more porous intellectual boundaries.

Science, but not superscience

The problem with the attempt by philosophers to treat the empirical scientist as a paradigm of intellectual virtue is that the astrophsyicist's love of truth seems no different from that of the classical philologist or the archive-orientated historian. All these people are trying hard to get something right. So, for that matter, are the master carpenter, the skilled accountant, and the careful surgeon. The need to get it right is central to all these people's sense of who they are, and what makes their lives worthwhile ... As I see it, our main job these days is to help convince the citizens of democratic communities that they will get no more political guidance from scientists and technologists than they got in the past from priests and philosophers.

(Richard Rorty, *Contingency, Irony, and Solidarity*)

It may surprise some readers that we have said so little about the New Pragmatism's relationship to natural science. There are two main reasons for this. First, as the philosopher of science Arthur Fine (1986: 116n.) has pointed out, scientists long ago forged ahead of those philosophers who theorize about their activities when it came to absorbing the pragmatist lesson that pure realism, based on the idea of confronting the world (e.g. for purposes of verification) *independently* of our ways of conceiving of it, is explanatorily empty.[26] Indeed, Fine's famous article "The Natural Ontological Attitude" kicks off by announcing "Realism is dead" (1986: 3).

On this understanding, the thought that science stands apart as the bastion of firm-minded, epistemic virtues that pragmatism foolhardily refuses to acknowledge and that other disciplines can normally only aspire to, is both philosophically old-fashioned and mistaken. Science is not the ultimate hard case that pragmatism butts up against at its own peril. And the virtues in question are better explained in pragmatist terms, specifying the appropriate social conditions of enquiry, and so forth, than those of the philosophical theorist who links scientific success with the single-minded pursuit of truth and assumes "that truth consists in the accurate representation of the intrinsic nature of reality" (Rorty 2000a: 105). Of course, if someone wanted to be clever about this, they could point out that scientists might not be the best judges of the nature of their own practices, and hence of what constitutes a good explanation of what it is they do. But, the New Pragmatist is inclined to ignore this sort of cleverness on the grounds that realism of the metaphysical variety favoured by philosophers seems to contribute nothing to scientific practice at ground level regardless of what scientists themselves tend to say about the matter, so issues concerning their competence to make higher-level judgements *about* that practice are irrelevant. Hence, since such realism has no practical value, it is of no particular philosophical interest.

The second reason for not singling out science for special attention follows on from the first. New Pragmatists do not make deep epistemically principled distinctions between disciplines. They see no sharp divide in this respect between natural science and, say, literature. Different disciplines use different vocabularies, for different purposes. They approach things differently on that account. A cognitive scientist takes a different approach to human consciousness from that of a novelist such as Henry James. Neither gets closer to what consciousness really is.

Moreover, as in the previous case, approaches may be so different that it is normally wrong to describe them as having a task in common (so usually we ought not to speak of the task of 'explaining' as if it is common to the activities of a cognitive scientist and a novelist with respect to their different accounts of consciousness). Sometimes disciplines overlap; sometimes the boundaries are redrawn; sometimes one discipline supplants another. But there are no grounds for making one discipline exemplary as such, irrespective of particular purposes: something for the others to always emulate. Pluralism reigns. For the New Pragmatist, this is how things are and how they should be. But, it does not usher in the sloppy forms of relativism that many critics of pragmatism, especially Rorty's brand, fear as strongly as they assume its inevitability. New Pragmatists can agree that certain disciplines are better suited for tackling certain tasks: that physics is better at predicting the motion of material bodies than, say, paranormal psychology. What they want to avoid, as Brandom rightly says of Rorty's "view towards science" (2000a: viii–ix), is a particular kind of misunderstanding of the value of domain-specific scientific discourses, practices and the attitudes they embody, one that affords them bogus intellectual priority over other discourses, practices and attitudes because they can supposedly generate a picture of reality that comes closer to what reality is really like than any other. Since science has no superior access to reality, philosophy's attempt to supplant it in order to become the uber-discipline was doomed from the start. There is no superscience.

CONCLUSION:
THE NEW PRAGMATISM
AND PHILOSOPHY

It is pictures rather than propositions, metaphors rather than
statements, which determine most of our philosophical convictions.   (Richard Rorty, *Philosophy and the Mirror of Nature*)

We have said that the New Pragmatism needs to capitalize on its
influence outside the field of philosophy itself. And, we have shown
some of the ways in which it has started to do so with enthusiasm
and evident accomplishment. Does this mean that it cannot flourish
within that field? This question needs to be split up. We did not intend
to imply that the New Pragmatism cannot do well within philosophy.
Our claim simply acknowledged that it would prefer to do well by its
own standards. And there is more social utility to be had, and more
scope for practical efficacy, if the New Pragmatism widens its sphere
of application. But, this still leaves untouched the question: can the
New Pragmatism do well within philosophy? What is there to say
about it?

Well, that question breaks down into the question of whether the
New Pragmatism is likely to succeed and a question about 'possibility': *can* it do so or is there good reason to think that philosophical
success is impossible? The first question is pretty straightforwardly
factual, and the answer depends on many contingent circumstances
and events that are difficult to predict. On the New Pragmatists'
side of things, much will depend on how creative they are in forging

alternative pictures of philosophical projects out of attractive images and metaphors: how good they are at following up on themes and questions that have already been introduced, and how good they are at thinking up new ones or sifting out those that promised more than they can deliver.

Creativity is an important factor here. Rorty was fond of telling us that in place of false goals such as 'truth' or 'a complete analysis of knowledge', philosophers should concentrate on thinking up new and interesting things to say. But notice that this advice lacks motivational force. Philosophers have said many fascinating things that turned out to be useful in ways that could not have been predicted but, more often that not, this was a by-product of the pursuit of an aim that Rorty would have regarded as having *itself* been discredited in pragmatism's eyes. Rorty's advice is useful as a handy test as to whether a philosophical project is, or was, worth pursuing, but it has little value as a prescription regarding what to set about doing in the first instance; it is about as useful as the advice 'buy low, sell high' in the investment world. As New Pragmatists let go of the traditional philosophical agenda and create their own by pursuing the kinds of alternative themes that are already attracting interest, such as the 'self-creation' theme we discussed in Chapter 3, new ideas will crop up and further questions will enflame their imaginations.

Besides motivation, there is also the question as to whether New Pragmatists will be able to make philosophical progress while tolerating differences of approach in their midst. There are many talented philosophers working within, and developing, various aspects of the New Pragmatism. But, they differ, for example, in their attitude to classic pragmatism, their assessment of rival traditions and even their response to the New Pragmatism's own founding figures, most notably Putnam and Rorty.

If we take Brandom and Misak, for instance, the former is influenced by, and sympathetic to, the work of Rorty, although not uncritically, whereas the latter objects to many of Rorty's views and is working towards what appears to be a more Peircean branch of the New Pragmatism (Misak 2009). Thus, although Misak claims "One, of the pillars of The New Pragmatism is the thought that standards of objectivity come into being and evolve over time, but that being historically situated in this way does not detract from their objectivity"

(2007: 2), she is sceptical as to whether Rorty's 'socialized' account of such standards can live up to this. By contrast, Brandom, building on his own early notion of the 'ontological priority of the social' (1983), wants to develop that account, although again not uncritically. Success for the New Pragmatism will greatly depend on whether it can continue to press ahead without getting bogged down in complex disputes over such differences within the fold.

On the other side, many philosophers, as we mentioned, are still highly resistant to pragmatism in any shape or form. Whether their resistance will prove to be an insurmountable barrier is difficult to tell. If it gains complete ascendancy and prevents academic courses on the New Pragmatism from being taught, if those who specialize in the New Pragmatism then find it difficult to get jobs, place articles in journals, have their written work sympathetically reviewed, their dissertations respected and so on, that could make it difficult for the New Pragmatism to establish a more stable and expansive presence within philosophy. Nevertheless, it could take off. Many philosophers, no doubt the vast majority, were until quite recently equally, if not more, hostile to continental philosophy. When I was a graduate student, Hegel, Nietzsche and Heidegger were openly mocked. Their texts were totally ignored, although occasionally used as philosophical dartboards. Now, Hegel's *The Phenomenology of Spirit*, Nietzsche's *The Genealogy of Morals* and Heidegger's *Being and Time* are probably more widely read and researched, even by philosophers, than Quine's *Word and Object*, Strawson's *Individuals*, Kripke's *Naming and Necessity*, and the other major works of analytical thinkers, with the exception, perhaps, of Wittgenstein who sits uneasily within that tradition in any case.

Of course, much of this depends on matters that the philosophers who resist the New Pragmatism would hasten to say have nothing to do with real success at all. Philosophical success depends on getting things right, not on popularity. So what about our further question: is it *possible* for the New Pragmatism to succeed within philosophy on philosophy's own terms? Again, the resisters would say no. And, they would say this for the reasons recorded in these pages: that the New Pragmatism is self-refuting; that its criterion of success, practical success, is no criterion at all and leads to sloppy relativism. But, New Pragmatists themselves believe that the common arguments

131

against their notion of success beg all the interesting questions and are carelessly unconscious of the contingency of their own underlying assumptions. So the question of prospects comes down in the end to one about defining the standards of success. And from that viewpoint – the viewpoint that such standards are up for grabs – there is nothing in the New Pragmatism, no conceptual failing, logical consistency, self-defeating relativistic tendency or whatever, that should prevent it from setting these standards, even within philosophy. Whether the New Pragmatists wish to haggle over such standards is another matter. If they agree with Rorty that philosophy deserves to enjoy no imperial powers, they may feel better satisfied by flourishing within culture and society at large, letting philosophy make of this what it may.

Finally, the way in which analytic philosophy interprets its own tradition will be an important factor in determining how much resistance it continues to mount against the New Pragmatism and how effective it will be in drawing people away from it. The analytic tradition has reached a stage where it is starting to pay closer attention to its own history. But so far it has tended to do so by way of proposing somewhat self-congratulatory accounts of that history. If, however, it starts to read its own texts with more self-critical awareness of how they relate to other texts outside the analytic tradition, and if it tackles them in the way that Rorty did, taking from philosophers such as Wittgenstein, Quine, Sellars and Davidson lessons in how to dismantle problem-generating methodologies and dissolve, or simply circumvent, the sorts of puzzles that keep their tradition alive, then the New Pragmatism may well gain some unexpected converts. Moreover, if other readers, those not already versed in the analytic tradition, come across passages in the same texts that appear to cast strong doubt on its viability, passages such as the following one from Wittgenstein's *The Blue and Brown Books*, they may well be receptive to the bad tidings and wonder why the analytic tradition has spent so much time fudging things in the face of them:

> For remember that in general we don't use language according to strict rules – it hasn't been taught us by means of strict rules, either. *We*, in our discussions on the other hand, constantly compare language with a calculus proceeding according to strict rules. This is a very one-sided way of looking at lan-

guage. In practice we very rarely use language as such a calculus. For not only do we not think of rules of usage – of definitions, etc. – while using language, but when we are asked to give such rules, in most cases we aren't able to do so. We are unable to clearly circumscribe the concepts we use; not because we don't know their real definition, but because there is no real 'definition' to them. To suppose that there *must* be would be like supposing that whenever children play with a ball they play a game according to strict rules ... Why then do we in philosophising constantly compare our use of words with one following strict rules? The answer is that the puzzles which we try to remove always spring from *just this attitude towards language.*

(1969: 25–6, emphasis added)

In this particular case, they are not likely to want to become one of those that Wittgenstein's "we" refers to. And they will be strongly disinclined to adopt the 'attitude towards language' he describes. Such readers will therefore tend to recoil from the embrace of much of the analytic tradition. They will shy away from some of the technical accomplishments it is most proud of. For they will be unable to see, for instance, why anyone would now want to write books advocating a formal linguistic approach to questions such as these:

How, we might ask, do ordinary speakers succeed in using elements of natural language (like English or Japanese) to convey meaning and communicate about the world and themselves? What kind of thing must an agent know to be a competent language user and what kind of cognitive architecture might be behind our linguistic abilities? (Borg 2004: 15)

New Pragmatists are usually suspicious of attempts to dig beneath the surface of social practices in order to locate some deeper structure, whether located in the mind or somewhere else, that will help explain those practices and their place in the world. Like Rorty, they tend to "see no more promise in inquiry into how mind and language work than into how conversation works" (2007: 181).[1]

The possibility that the New Pragmatism could play some sort of restraining role, keeping philosophy engrossed in surface practicalities and subsequent pay-offs, is one that analytic philosophers seem to fear too much in anticipation to cooperate with. Nevertheless, this could be another way in which the New Pragmatism expands its area of influence to the common good. For by asking analytic philosophers to meet pragmatic criteria of success, New Pragmatists could provide a useful external check on their projects. Leaving aside the semantics industry and all those ancillary workers trying to construct related mental maps, think of the amount of time and energy that is still spent in trying to throw the mantle of systematic moral theory over the whole of human life, leaving no unruly residue untouched. Those involved in this kind of venture are inclined to tinker around with received notions, trying for instance to finesse the nature of obligations or square everything in the hurly burly of moral life with the demands of Kantian versions of rationality while, all the time, sitting quietly on top of some unchallenged background assumptions (e.g. that there is a sharp distinction between prudence and morality or that moral agents are best described non-relationally – as if moral concern for others is essentially an extrinsic feature of their self-identity, and they need (self-interested) reasons to activate it). To be asked practical questions – questions such as 'What is the practical value of all this tinkering?', 'What is the practical basis for this particular distinction?', 'What do we gain, in practical terms, by separating reasons out for special attention?', 'Would things go worse, practically speaking, if we gave up using this (theoretical) term and used that (practical) one instead?' – could help moral theorists to converse with those outside their narrowly circumscribed moral-theoretical universe, the one inhabited by fellow thinkers and tinkers such as Socrates, Kant, Mill, Hare, Mackie and Parfit. They might thereby learn to better explain the value of their line of thinking and tinkering. In some cases, perhaps many, such questioning, if pursued far enough, is likely to reduce the theorists' ambitions, if not put a stop to them altogether.[2]

Furthermore, if the analytic tradition has the integrity and insight to heed the voices within its own ranks that have been telling it to shut up shop on many of its preoccupations, the fresh concerns of the New Pragmatism will seem all the more attractive and are likely to bloom even more brightly. Readers who find James's *Pragmatism* endlessly stimulating, if rather quaint, and who find they are unable to kick off their philosophical education with standard texts like Russell's *Problems of Philosophy* or Nagel's *What Does It All Mean?* because they simply cannot swallow the presuppositions that leap out from behind the barrier of seemingly plain-dealing prose that is supposed to hide them, will then realize they have something very worthwhile to turn to.

NOTES

Preface

1. Rorty deliberately excluded Peirce, the first of pragmatism's three founding figures. This is a bone of contention with Rorty's critics, and others who want to see old-style pragmatism given much more philosophical credit.

1. Introducing the New Pragmatism

1. "The revival of pragmatism has excited enormous interest and controversy in the intellectual community over the past two decades" (Dickstein 1998: 1).
2. Even relatively recent accounts continue to foster this image. Witness Howard Mounce: "Pragmatism is the distinctively American philosophy" (1997: 1).
3. Classic pragmatism made initial progress on the international front, but was unable to sustain its impact. For a brief overview of its early achievements in this respect, see Shook (2009).
4. The Bibliography lists some of the relevant writings of these philosophers. A full list would include thinkers outside the field of philosophy.
5. For example, 'What is justice?', 'What is knowledge?', 'What is truth?', and so forth. Cf. "It never occurs to us even later that the question 'what is *the* truth?' is not a real question" (PMT: 115–16).
6. Cornel West points out that thinkers such as Frederic Jameson, Hal Foster and Andreas Huyssen extend the boundaries of the postmodern debate: "Instead of viewing 'Postmodernism' as a set of styles, sensibilities, or viewpoints, they posit [it] as a social category, a cultural dominant" (West 1989: 237).
7. We should not underestimate the extent of this "seepage". Just last night, I watched a character in the very popular television show *The Sopranos* put

down the book he was reading, and it turned out to be Robert Nozick's *Anarchy, State, and Utopia*. Academic publishers have certainly started to recognize this phenomenon; witness the recent Wiley-Blackwell series of books entitled *X and Philosophy*, where X denotes a well-known television programme.

8. Here we need to be quite careful. The New Pragmatism *does* blend with the overall intellectual ethos, and much of postmodernist thinking in particular, but it faces sharp resistance from the dominant *philosophical* approach, namely, that of analytic philosophy.

9. It should, however, be noted that there has been a campaign, started by Rorty, to pragmatize as many of these thinkers as possible.

10. "Knowingness is a state of soul which prevents shudders of awe. It makes one immune to romantic enthusiasm" (Rorty 1998a: 126).

11. Many of its critics, however, either fail to see this or deny that it is possible (because the debate in question is all-embracing).

12. We revisit this in Chapter 4. See also: "Philosophy is inherently criticism, having its distinctive position among various modes of criticism in its generality; a criticism of criticisms, as it were" (EN: 38).

13. Putnam claims that it is James's way of thinking about "hard issues" rather than his solutions to them that he finds "inspiring" (POQ: 22). In the same book, he takes heart from Dewey's opposition to "the philosophers' habit of dichotomization" (*ibid.*: 73). Rorty frequently acknowledges that both Dewey and James had a liberating influence on his own philosophical thought without needing to provide him with much by way of doctrine or methodology.

14. James said this in 1905. At the same time, James also said he believed "a new kind of dawn is breaking upon us philosophers" (PMT: 10).

15. Since writing this, I have noticed that Richard Bernstein makes a similar point in "Pragmatism, Pluralism and the Healing of Wounds", reprinted in Bernstein (1992: 334).

16. Putnam's views appear to have moved closer to Rorty's of late in the sense that he finds less and less of value in analytic philosophy. However, he is still very reluctant to join with Rorty in recommending that philosophers set aside virtually the whole of that tradition.

17. As we shall discover in Chapter 3, Rorty was never comfortably ensconced within the analytic tradition, however, and the common perception that he suddenly betrayed it in *Philosophy and the Mirror of Nature* is mistaken.

18. "Rorty's historicism has had such an explosive force because he attacked the citadel of philosophy from within" (Kloppenberg 1998: 91).

19. And 'futile' for various reasons: that pragmatism was outmoded, something of historical interest at best; that Dewey was a long-winded, boring thinker who had failed to keep up with the philosophical developments of his time; and so forth.

2. Leaving classic pragmatism behind

1. See, for example, Susan Haack's (1997) fierce objections to Louis Menand's (1997) interpretation of classic pragmatism's origins where she claims that he both misinterprets and downgrades Peirce's role.
2. James later pointed out that the term 'pragmatism' derives from the Greek word for action, "from which our words 'practice' and 'practical' come" (PMT: 28).
3. It is difficult to assess the significance of this. But the points we make hold regardless of Peirce's personal circumstances.
4. James's writings on psychology and religion had philosophical content, but it is unlikely that they would have had much impact in the field of philosophy in their own right. Even Wittgenstein's interest in them, for example, has sparked little serious interest in that respect.
5. James was not keen on the term 'pragmatism' and would have preferred to follow Schiller by using 'humanism' instead. Ironically, he chose 'pragmatism' out of respect for Peirce, who came to dislike it so much, as we pointed out, that he abandoned it.
6. John Murphy says that James's *Pragmatism* "is the book that spread Pragmatism around the world" (1990: 39).
7. Rorty's definition of 'scientism' is also to the point here: "By 'scientism' I mean the doctrine that natural science is privileged over other areas of culture, that something about natural science puts it in closer – or at least more reliable – touch with reality than any other human activity" (Rorty 1998b: 294).
8. For a useful discussion of Dewey's approach to science, see Mounce (1997: 144–57).
9. Some critics claim that Dewey underestimated the role that abstract theorizing plays in science; see, for example, Cohen (1940).
10. We discuss some of the criticisms alluded to here in Chapter 4. See also Malachowski (2004b).
11. In this connection, Rorty distinguishes between Dewey "the prophet, the Emersonian visionary" and Dewey "the contributor to *The Journal of Philosophy* who spent 40 years haggling over definitions of 'true'" (2000a 96–7). James T. Kloppenberg says of James and Dewey that "some of their best writing came in response to their critics" (1998: 85). He refers, in particular, to *The Meaning of Truth* and *Experience and Nature*, but fails to consider the possibilities that such responses came at a high cost in terms of creativity and that they were counterproductive in the sense that they dignified some ill-considered or rather frivolous criticisms with a seriousness they did not deserve.
12. See "Dewey Between Hegel and Darwin", in Rorty (1998b: 290–306). For a rejoinder to Rorty that tries, unsuccessfully in my view, to show that Dewey's idea of "immediate experience" can be useful when stripped of its "foundationalist function", see Shusterman (1999).
13. Cf. Dewey: "The Pragmatist holds that the relation in question [i.e. of 'agreement' or 'correspondence'] is one of correspondence between existence and thought" (1910: 5).

14. See "Wittgenstein and the Linguistic Turn", in Rorty (2007: 160–75).
15. Some analytic philosophers, however, most notably perhaps Thomas Nagel, have still generated a problematic around the supposedly irreducible notion of conscious experience.
16. This means "medium of representation in a *philosophical* sense", the sense that generates the whole mind–world problematic. The New Pragmatism does not deny that the notion of representation makes perfect sense *within* ordinary language use, as in "That portrait of Obama is a good representation of the President".
17. We should mention that the New Pragmatism has two neoteric aspects. First, under the impetus of the work of Putnam and Rorty, it has shed some layers of the dead philosophical skin that weighed classic pragmatism down. Secondly, aided by this shedding, philosophers such as Bjørn Ramberg and Robert Brandom have been busy updating it. The New Pragmatism is a work in progress. It is also worth mentioning that knee-jerk reactions to pragmatist views ignore what has been done in this respect, and thus tend to keep beating up on straw targets.
18. For an example of someone going back to classic pragmatism for inspiration independently of the New Pragmatism, see Mayorga (2008).

3. Rorty against the tradition

1. Ample evidence of the vitality of this 'interest' can be found in Rorty (2000a).
2. Brandom is referring to Rorty's eliminative materialism and his notion of incorrigibility.
3. For a more detailed overview of *Philosophy and the Mirror of Nature*, see Malachowski (2006).
4. This is not the place to go into details, but it should be noted that when Rorty's critics complain about some of his views, they seem to overlook the fact that he derived them from *within* the analytic tradition itself, from thinkers whose radical nature they also seem to have somehow overlooked.
5. Notice that this conflates knowledge and experience, as if there can be no appearance–reality distinction within the mind's own domain. This has historical consequences that we cannot go into here. But, if it sparks off some questioning thoughts, see, for example, the discussion of Saul Kripke's famous treatment of pain in connection with mind–body identity theory in Fitch (2004: 132–5).
6. These two formulations are not strictly equivalent. They raise different issues, but they can be equated here for brevity's sake.
7. This speculation is reinforced by Rorty's biographical remarks, where he claims to have been concerned from the start that philosophers may never be able to furnish objective, non-circular justification of their views. See Rorty (2000a: 3–20).

8. There are plans to publish them in collected format, although these are provisional and, as yet, no publication date is available.
9. There are some exceptions. These include Rorty's outline of his conception of pragmatism in *Philosophy and Social Hope* (2000a: 23–90). For insightful attempts to make something more systematic of Rorty's approach to pragmatism, see Brodsky ([1982] 2004) and Kraut (2004).
10. Having said that, Rorty made concerted attempts to engage with his critics, but one never gets the sense that he is backtracking when doing so. His primary purpose of breaking free of the past is also evident in those exchanges.
11. For some elaboration of this point see Malachowski (2004b).

4. Putnam's contributions

1. The best book on Putnam's philosophy in general is de Gaynesford (2006).
2. See typical Peircian remarks such as "If philosophy is ever to become a sound science ..." and "This maxim [that a concept is explicable in terms of its 'conceivable practical consequences'] is put forth neither as a handy tool to serve so far as may be found serviceable, nor as a self-evident truth, but as a far-reaching theorem solidly grounded upon an elaborate study of the nature of signs" (Peirce 1904, reprinted in Menand 1997: 56–7). Susan Haack is prominent among those who deny that Peirce's approach to philosophy was scientistic. But even so she occasionally says things that can be interpreted scientistically. Furthermore, David Hollinger is surely right to point out that "Peirce was unusual – even in an age of extravagant 'scientism' – in the extremity and singularity with which he identified goodness and progress with science" (Hollinger 1995: 22).
3. A good case could be made for claiming that Rorty had a similarly galvanizing effect on Heidegger studies. Many analytic philosophers who avoided Heidegger on the superficial say-so of hostile critics such as Carnap became curious enough to explore his work when Rorty made him one of the three heroes of *Philosophy and the Mirror of Nature*. And some of these were pleasantly surprised by what they discovered there.
4. Kloppenberg rightly observes that James "simply took for granted" the existence of an independent reality "and did not consider its independent existence philosophically interesting or important" (1998: 86).
5. Putnam regards 'direct realism', for example, as an "implicit and everyday conviction" rather than "a particular metaphysical theory" (see Putnam 1995b: 37).
6. This is from "The Pragmatist account of Truth and its Misunderstanders" (PMT: 265–82).
7. He objects, for example, to the implication, on his interpretation of James, that the truth of all statements about the past depends on their being believed at some time in the future (see EWO: 136–7).

8. 'Beyond' because he is sceptical that the main philosophical problems provoked by such dualisms can be resolved.

9. Putnam is not against 'abstraction' in itself. In "Pragmatism and Moral Objectivity" he acknowledges that "positions on the 'abstract' question of moral objectivity have real world effects" (in Putnam 1995b: 151). His disenchantment with analytic philosophy stems from its tendency to generate and focus on problems whose importance and interest have become largely internal to that tradition. James was similarly insistent that pragmatism is not opposed to abstraction *per se*.

10. "I am inclined to say that James speaks from inside the philosophical tradition, he takes its problems seriously; his answers, to be sure, lead him beyond the tradition. In contrast, when he wrote his later works, Dewey had already achieved a position outside the tradition" (R. A. Putnam 1998: 70).

11. "Much of present education fails because it neglects [the] fundamental principle of school as a form of community life" (LW 11: 446).

12. Interestingly, Dewey is frequently criticized for having an insufficiently substantial account of the self, but such criticisms tend to rely on precisely the kind of traditional assumptions about the self that Dewey was keen to avoid.

13. Critics who pounce on Rorty for saying that if freedom is taken care of, then truth will take care of itself (typically, on the nit-picking grounds that there is no tight connection between freedom and truth), seem to be unaware that he is alluding to this much more complex Deweyan picture.

14. "Freedom of thought in inquiry and in dissemination of the conclusions of inquiry is the vital nerve of democratic institutions" (LW 11: 375).

15. Here we closely follow Westbrook's exposition, which is, for our introductory purposes, more perspicuous than Putnam's own.

16. Westbrook also cites Dewey's contention that "A class of experts is inevitably so removed from common interests as to become a class with private interests and private knowledge, which in social matters is not knowledge at all" (Westbrook 1998: 132).

17. This is not to say that the term the 'New Pragmatists' is original (we acknowledged this much in the Preface), but only that when it has been used by others, its status as a name has not been fully endorsed or even acknowledged, and that it has not yet 'caught on' in that sense.

5. Putnam and Rorty: pragmatism without reconciliation

1. To review the debate in its entirety would take at least a book in itself, and indeed would make a very worthwhile project.

2. Rorty finds this fault in a number of other philosophers, most notably Quine, although Quine is also rebuked for failing to follow through on the implications of some of his own views (see PMN: 192–209). For Quine's objections to Rorty's take on him, see Quine (1990).

3. One of the most frequent charges made against Rorty is that his views either embed or entail irrationality.
4. Claims that Rorty was unable to avail himself of everyday locutions – 'The map represents the territory', and so on – are still commonly made in criticism of him. Such criticisms often exhibit a peculiar pattern: first, Rorty's position is outlined in a crude form; then some non-philosophical considerations are adduced as evidence of the incoherence of that position (considerations such as 'It makes sense to say that such and such an account of X accurately represents how things are with X'); then, as a fait accompli, the original metaphysical views that Rorty was objecting to are resurrected, as if these considerations lend it credibility even as they take it away from him. The move is reminiscent of attempts to refute scepticism by appealing to sensible uses of 'I know'. But, it is even less appropriate because Rorty, following the classic pragmatists, never ruled against ordinary uses of 'represents'. For an example of this ploy, although one that is more sophisticated and much better informed than usual, see Blackburn (2006a: 151–71).

6. Prospects

1. This is not to imply that such disputes are deliberately kept going in full consciousness that they are good for no other purpose than keeping philosophers in business. There are various elements of self-deception that we need not speculate on here.
2. Thus, for instance, it is noticeable that when someone takes Rorty's views seriously, they are often accused of favouring irrationality, as if analytic philosophy has proprietary rights over what is and is not 'rational'. From the New Pragmatist's perspective, the situation is reversed: it is rational to advocate belief in something when all the evidence suggests it is true while remaining open to the possibility that it might turn out to be false and it is the view there is something metaphysically vital missing here, something transcending all evidence and epistemic social practice considerations, that lacks a rational basis.
3. It also has the advantage, that we need not dwell on here, of specifically aiming to confer practical benefits. More theoretical approaches, of which applied analytic philosophy is the paradigm case, tend to lose sight of this aim and often end up turning practical difficulties into intractable conceptual problems.
4. See, for example, the report in the *New York Times* on Columbia University's 1999 conference on pragmatism and architecture (Boxer 2000) and Cocks & Reveley (2007).
5. Alert readers will perhaps have noticed some vagueness, and even ambiguity, in the discussion so far. We speak of 'areas' rather than 'disciplines' and of 'literature', 'feminism' and so on, rather than, say, 'literary theory', feminist studies', and so on. This is deliberate. And, the reason is that, in many cases, the New Pragmatism has tended to have an impact not only on intellectual

disciplines but also, as it were, on the subject matter they deal with; so, for instance, it has not influenced just the ways in which novels and poems are studied and subjected to theoretical scrutiny, but also the ways in which they are written. All of this is, of course, to be expected of a philosophical approach that is concerned to break down the barriers between theory and practice. For instructive illustrations as to how this has panned out with regard to architecture, for example, see the chapter entitled "New Pragmatism" in *21st Century House* (Bell 2002).

6. This is a substantial empirical claim. But as an assiduous reader of philosophical journals and books as well as poetry and literature in general, I have been able to personally witness a sea-change in attitudes towards this relationship, and from both sides of it. A relationship that was once ignored or derided now has a thriving industry devoted to celebrating and exploring its possibilities.

7. I say 'imagine' because scientists themselves were generally unimpressed, if not hostile.

8. In a previous draft, I spoke of Rorty 'coming to the rescue' here, and was rightly chastised for doing so by an anonymous reviewer. I should have recalled Rorty's own wry insistence that part of a pragmatist's progress involves abandoning "daydreams in which the heroic pragmatist plays a Walter Mitty-like role in the immanent teleology of world history" (2000a: 133–4). This is still an idealized account, but I need make no further apologies for it. Rorty's interventions had a tremendous impact in stirring up renewed interest in literature. Even when they disagreed with him, critics were prompted to view things afresh and consider renascent possibilities.

9. See Rorty's article with that title, as reprinted in Rorty (1998b: 125–40).

10. For an insightful discussion of the tensions between self-transformation and social change in Rorty's approach to literature, see "The Politics of the Novel" in Voparil (2006: 61–88).

11. For an incisive account of this theme in Plato's *Republic*, see Blackburn (2006b: 149–57).

12. According to Luban, these include: "a behaviourist treatment of mental states, a soft determinism about free will, a moderate scepticism in epistemology, and an economic conception of rationality" (1998: 277; see Posner 1998).

13. For a useful summary of the 'intersections' between classic pragmatism and feminism, see Sullivan (2009).

14. No doubt Rorty had Dewey in mind here: "Social arrangements are not means for obtaining something for individuals ... They are means for *creating* individuals" (RP: 122).

15. Wain is referring to Rorty (2000a: 114–26).

16. For an insightful overview, see Festenstein (1997).

17. Most notably by Cheryl Misak (2000). For an astute account of the state of play regarding the 'epistemological argument', see Westbrook (2009).

18. No doubt he also had Marxism in mind here.

19. Notice the emphasis here, again, on language. This was deliberate. Rorty argued that linguistic ability is the only thing that is distinctive about human

beings. However, he conceded that other art forms could play a correlative role, and claimed that it was just ignorance on his part that prevented him from talking about them. Presumably, when pressed, he would have contended that linguistic awareness would have to come into play within these other art forms at some stage.

20. For an informative summary of these developments, see Frankenberry (2009).

21. For more on this, see Malachowski (2002b).

22. There are many reasons why the distinction between the 'analytic tradition' and the 'continental tradition' is unsatisfactory, but it marks out the boundaries of a dispute between different conceptions of philosophy that, in the end, depend on which philosophers are believed to be important and hence worth reading. Although others have done this, Rorty put pressure on these boundaries by showing how it is profitable to combine readings of philosophers who supposedly belong on different sides of them (e.g. Heidegger and Wittgenstein).

23. I say 'apotheoisis' because one of Derrida's unique achievements seems to have been to leave other thinkers wondering what to do next by way of moving beyond him. Of course, this stalemate is only temporary.

24. Here I mean 'stopped reading' in the sense that they no longer expect to learn anything from such texts and therefore fail to pay them any respectful attention.

25. I am somewhat light-heartedly alluding to Derrida's practice of deploying words such as 'Being' with a line drawn through them.

26. This is not to say that science absorbed the lesson directly *from* pragmatism. Its historical relationship to pragmatism remains to be told.

Conclusion: the New Pragmatism and philosophy

1. All this is rather swift. For further elaboration of Rorty's suspicions that extends them to cover the whole project in the philosophy of language of devising theories of meaning, truth and so forth, and that does so on precisely the kinds of Wittgensteinian grounds we allude to, see his opening remarks in a discussion with Donald Davidson (www.youtube.com/watch?v=EjWTuF35GtY), especially where he speaks of learning a language in the way that one learns to ride a bicycle. And, for a more considered treatment of analytic philosophy's "epic confrontation with Wittgensteinian Pragmatism", see Brandom (2008). In identifying the "displacement from the centre of philosophical attention of *meaning* in favour of *use*" and a correlative replacement of "concern with *semantics* by concern with *pragmatics*", Brandom opens up the possibility of a reconciliation between analytic philosophy and the New Pragmatism. We do not explore this possibility because its complexities are not suitable for treatment in an introductory text. Furthermore, it involves a seismic shift in analytic philosophers' perception of the historical roots of their approach

to philosophy, one that seems unlikely to occur in the near future given their staunch resistance to Rorty's attempts to push them in that direction. However, should such a shift take place, The New Pragmatism could flourish *within* philosophy itself by more or less appropriating it or, more stealthily, by letting itself be appropriated. For more on this, see "Are we all Pragmatists Now?" (Malachowski 2010c).

2. For examples of Rorty's debunking of the grand ambitions of moral theorists, see "Kant vs. Dewey: The Current Situation of Moral Philosophy", in Rorty (2007: 184–202).

READING THE NEW PRAGMATISTS

Advice on reading the New Pragmatists needs to be sensitive to the 'Why?' behind the project. For those who simply want to find out more about these thinkers and their style of philosophy, it is probably best to recapitulate the structure of this book. First, for purposes of contrast, take a closer look at the classic pragmatists, then move on to the writings of Rorty and Putnam, and, finally, explore some of New Pragmatist work in broader areas of interest and at the cutting edge of the development of its own ideas. The following section offers suggestions for taking the first two steps on this path; the final step can be taken in the company of those who feel they already know enough to require a more sophisticated agenda.

Classic pragmatism

The secondary literature is now vast, and still proliferating at speed. A fair proportion is of dubious quality, but there is no substitute for starting with the primary texts in any case. Here are some basic references for the collected works of Peirce, James and Dewey:

Collected Papers of Charles S. Peirce, 8 vols, C. Hartshorne, P. Weiss & A. Burks (eds) (Cambridge, MA: Harvard University Press, 1931–58).
The Works of William James, 18 vols, F. Burkhardt, F. Bowers & I. Skrupskelis (eds) (Cambridge, MA: Harvard University Press, 1975–88).
The Collected Works of John Dewey, 1882–1953, 37 vols, J. Boydston (ed.) (Carbondale, IL: Southern Illinois University Press, 1969–90).

There are also a number of useful anthologies that have substantial selections from the three classic pragmatists we have focused on as well as others. The most notable are Malachowski (2004a), Menand (1997) and S. Haack & R. Lane (eds), *Pragmatism Old and New: Selected Writings* (New York: Prometheus, 2006).

Among the extensive secondary literature, Shook & Margolis (2009) and the following provide instructive starting-points and plenty of rich food for thought thereafter:

M. Bauerlein & J. Stuhr (eds), *100 Years of Pragmatism: William James's Revolutionary Philosophy* (Bloomington, IN: Indiana University Press, 2008).

R. Gale, *The Philosophy of William James: An Introduction* (Cambridge: Cambridge University Press, 2004).

C. Haskins & D. Seiple (eds), *Dewey Reconfigured* (Albany, NY: SUNY Press, 1999).

C. Hookway, *Peirce* (London: Routledge, 1985).

A. Malachowski (ed.), *The Cambridge Companion to Pragmatism* (Cambridge: Cambridge University Press, 2010).

R. A. Putnam (ed.), *The Cambridge Companion to William James* (Cambridge: Cambridge University Press, 2008).

On Quine

The philosophical ideas of Quine and Davidson can be painlessly accessed through the corresponding chapters in C. Belshaw & G. Kemp (eds), *Twelve Modern Philosophers* (Oxford: Wiley-Blackwell, 2009). For more detailed treatments that connect up well with the material in this book, see A. Orenstein, *W. V. Quine* (Chesham: Acumen, 2002) and B. Ramberg, *Donald Davidson: Philosophy of Language* (Oxford: Blackwell, 1991).

On Rorty and Putnam

For more detailed discussion of Rorty's approach to pragmatism, see especially Brodsky ([1982] 2004), Kraut (2004) and H. Saatkamp (ed.), *Rorty and Pragmatism: The Philosopher Responds to his Critics* (Nashville, TN: Vanderbilt University Press, 1995).

For discussion and exploration of Rorty's philosophy as a whole, the following are useful: Brandom (2000a); Festenstein & Thompson (2001); Guignon & Hiley (2003); Malachowski (1990, 2002a,b); Saatkamp, *Rorty and Pragmatism*; Voparil (2006); and N. Gascoigne, *Richard Rorty: Liberalism, Irony, and the Ends of Philosophy* (Cambridge: Polity, 2008).

Some of the best material on Putnam's treatment of pragmatism is to be found in J. Conant & U. Zegleu (eds), *Hilary Putnam: Pragmatism and Realism* (London: Routledge, 2006). On Putnam's overall philosophy, see: De Gaynesford (2006); C. Norris, *Hilary Putnam: Realism, Reason and the Uses of Uncertainty*

(Manchester: Manchester University Press, 2002); and Y. Ben-Menahem (ed.), *Hilary Putnam* (Cambridge: Cambridge University Press, 2005).

Further explorations for philosophy experts and others

For an overview of New Pragmatists at work in areas outside philosophy, see Dickstein (1998). To get a feel for New Pragmatists at work in their most sophisticated mode, developing pragmatist ideas, resituating them with regard to the analytic tradition or reinterpreting the writings of other New Pragmatists, see: Brandom (1994, 2000b, 2008); Ramberg (2000, 2009); and D. Macarthur & H. Price, "Pragmatism, Quasi-realism, and the Global Challenge", in Misak (2007), 91–121.

Some of the material here will be found congenial to those who can only stomach pragmatism if it preserves the virtues of analytic philosophy or can somehow be made compatible with it. Of course, those requirements conflict with the more dismissive line taken in the main text here. It suggests that many of analytic philosophy's traditional concerns are best sidestepped, and that its virtues of clarity, rigour in argumentation and so on, such as they are, are not unique to it. But to mount a defence against the coming encroachment of analytic philosophy will require another instalment.

BIBLIOGRAPHY

Arcilla, R. 1990. "Edification, Conversation, and Narrative: Rortyan Motifs for Philosophy of Education". *Educational Theory* **40**(1): 35–9.

Bakhurst, D. 2007. "Pragmatism and Ethical Particularism". In *New Pragmatists*, C. Misak (ed.), 122–41. Oxford: Clarendon Press.

Bell, J. 2002. *21st Century House*. London: Laurence King.

Bernstein, R. 1992. *The New Constellation*. Cambridge, MA: MIT Press.

Bird, A. 2009. "Kripke". Reprinted in *Twelve Modern Philosophers*, C. Belshaw & G. Kemp (eds), 151–72. Oxford: Wiley-Blackwell.

Blackburn, S. 2006a. *Truth*. Oxford: Oxford University Press.

Blackburn, S. 2006b. *Plato's Republic: A Biography*. London: Atlantic.

Borg, E. 2004. *Minimal Semantics*. Oxford: Oxford University Press.

Boxer, S. 2000. "The New Face of Architecture". *New York Times* (25 November). www.nytimes.com/2000/11/25/arts/the-new-face-of-architecture.html?pagewanted=all (accessed October 2009).

Brandom, R. 1983. "Heidegger's Categories in *Being and Time*". *The Monist* **66**(3): 387–409.

Brandom, R. 1994. *Making it Explicit*. Cambridge, MA: Harvard University Press.

Brandom, R. (ed.) 2000a. *Rorty and his Critics*. Oxford: Blackwell.

Brandom, R. 2000b. "Vocabularies of Pragmatism: Synthesising Naturalism and Historicism". See Brandom (2000a), 156–83.

Brandom, R. 2008. *Between Saying and Doing: Towards an Analytic Pragmatism*. Oxford: Oxford University Press.

Brodsky, G. [1982] 2004. "Rorty's Interpretation of Pragmatism". See Malachowski (2004a), vol. 3, 194–211.

Brueckner, A. [1983] 2002. "Transcendental Arguments I". Reprinted in *Richard Rorty*, 4 vols, A. Malachowski (ed.), vol. 1, 127–42. London: Sage.

Burke, T. 1998. *Dewey's New Logic: A Reply to Russell*. Chicago, IL: University of Chicago Press.

Cocks, R. & J. Reveley 2007. "Pragmatism, Music and Emotion: Bridging the Organisational Aesthetics Subject–Object Divide". *International Journal of Work Organisation and Emotion* **2**(2): 129–44.

Cohen, M. R. 1940. "Some Difficulties in Dewey's Anthropocentric Naturalism". *Philosophical Review* **49**: 9–10.

De Gaynesford, M. 2006. *Hilary Putnam*. Chesham: Acumen.

Dewey, J. 1910. "A Short Catechism Concerning Truth". In his *The Influence of Darwin on Philosophy and Other Essays*, 154–68. New York: Henry Holt.

Dewey, J. 1916. *Democracy and Education*. New York: Macmillan.

Dewey, J. 1920. *Reconstruction in Philosophy*. New York: Macmillan.

Dewey, J. 1958. *Experience and Nature*. New York: Dover.

Dewey, J. 1981–2008. *The Collected Works of John Dewey: The Later Works*. Carbondale, IL: Southern Illinois University Press.

Dewey, J. 2004. "The Development of American Pragmatism". See Malachowski (2004a), vol. 1, 3–17.

Dickstein, M. (ed.) 1998. *The Revival of Pragmatism: New Essays on Social Thought, Law, and Culture*. Durham, NC: Duke University Press.

Festenstein, M. 1997. *Pragmatism and Political Theory: From Dewey to Rorty*. Chicago, IL: University of Chicago Press.

Festenstein, M. 2001. "Pragmatism, Social Democracy and Practical Argument". In *Richard Rorty: Political Dialogues*, M. Festenstein & S. Thompson (eds), 203–18. Cambridge: Polity.

Festenstein, M. & S. Thompson (eds) 2001. *Richard Rorty: Political Dialogues*. Cambridge: Polity.

Fine, A. 1986. "The Natural Ontological Attitude". In his *The Shaky Game: Einstein, Realism and the Quantum Theory*, 112–35. Chicago, IL: University of Chicago Press.

Fitch, G. 2004. *Saul Kripke*. Chesham: Acumen.

Forster, P. [1992] 2004. "What is at Stake Between Putnam and Rorty?" See Malachowski (2004a), vol. 3, 57–76.

Frankenberry, N. 2009. "Religious Empiricism and Naturalism". See Shook & Margolis (2009), 221–30.

Grey, T. 1998. "Freestanding Legal Pragmatism". See Dickstein (1998), 254–74.

Guignon, C. & D. Hiley (eds) 2003. *Richard Rorty*. Cambridge: Polity.

Gunn, G. 1995. "Rethinking the Deweyan Legacy". In *Pragmatism: From Progressivism to Postmodernism*, R. Hollinger & D. Depew (eds), 298–313. Westport, CT: Praeger.

Haack, S. 1997. "Vulgar Rortyism". *New Criterion* **16** (November): 67.

Hollinger, R. 1995. "The Problem of Pragmatism in American History: A Look Back and a Look Ahead". In *Pragmatism: From Progressivism to Postmodernism*, R. Hollinger & D. Depew (eds), 19–37. Westport, CT: Praeger.

Hollinger, R. & D. Depew (eds) 1995. *Pragmatism: From Progressivism to Postmodernism*. Westport, CT: Praeger.

James, W. 1970. *Essays in Pragmatism*. New York: Free Press.

James, W. 1996. *Essays in Radical Empiricism*. Lincoln, NE: University of Nebraska Press.

James, W. 1998. *Pragmatism and The Meaning of Truth*. Cambridge, MA: Harvard University Press.

Keats, J. 1988. *Collected Poems*. Harmondsworth: Penguin.

Kloppenberg, J. T. 1998. "Pragmatism: An Old Name for Some New Ways of Thinking". See Dickstein (1998), 83–127.

Kraut, R. 2004. "Varieties of Pragmatism". See Malachowski (2004a), vol. 2, 260–84.

Larkin, P. 1998. *Collected Poems*. London: Faber.

Luban, D. 1998. "What's Pragmatic about Legal Pragmatism?" See Dickstein (1988), 275–303.

Magnus, B. 1995. "Postmodern Pragmatism: Nietzsche, Heidegger, Derrida, and Rorty". In *Pragmatism: From Progressivism to Postmodernism*, R. Hollinger & D. Depew (eds), 256–83. Westport, CT: Praeger.

Malachowski, A. (ed.) 1990. *Reading Rorty*. Oxford: Blackwell.

Malachowski, A. (ed.) 2002a. *Richard Rorty*, 4 vols. London: Sage.

Malachowski, A. 2002b. *Richard Rorty*. Chesham: Acumen.

Malachowski, A. (ed.) 2004a. *Pragmatism*, 3 vols. London: Sage.

Malachowski, A. 2004b. "Pragmatism in its Own Right". See Malachowski (2004a), vol. 2, 337–42.

Malachowski, A. 2006. "Richard Rorty: *Philosophy and the Mirror of Nature*". In *Central Works of Philosophy 5: The Twentieth Century: Quine and After*, J. Shand (ed.), 126–45. Chesham: Acumen.

Malachowski, A. 2010a. *The Cambridge Companion to Pragmatism*. Cambridge: Cambridge University Press.

Malachowski, A. 2010b. "The Human Continuum: James's Holism". See Malachowski (2010a).

Malachowski, A. 2010c. "Are we all Pragmatists Now?" See Malachowski (2010a).

Margolis, J. 2009. "Introduction". See Shook & Margolis (2009), 1–10.

Mayorga, R. M. M. 2008. "Rethinking Democratic Ideals in the Light of Charles Peirce". *Contemporary Pragmatism* **5**(2): 1–10.

Menand, L. (ed.) 1997. *Pragmatism: A Reader*. New York: Vintage.

Misak, C. 2000. *Truth, Politics, Morality: Pragmatism and Deliberation*. London: Routledge.

Misak, C. (ed.) 2007. *New Pragmatists*. Oxford: Clarendon Press.

Misak, C. 2009. "Scientific Realism, Anti-Realism, and Empiricism". See Shook & Margolis (2009), 398–409.

Moore, G. E. [1907] 1960. "William James's Pragmatism". In his *Philosophical Studies*, 97–146. London: Routledge.

Mounce, H. O. 1997. *The Two Pragmatisms: From Peirce to Rorty*. London: Routledge.

Munitz, M. K. 1981. *Contemporary Analytic Philosophy*. New York: Macmillan.

Murphy, J. 1990. *Pragmatism: From Peirce to Davidson*. Boulder, CO: Westview.

Nicholson, C. 1989. "Postmodernism, Feminism, and Education: The Need for Solidarity". *Educational Theory* **39**(3): 197–205.

Pattison, G. 2000. *The Later Heidegger*. London: Routledge.

Peirce, C. S. 1955. *Philosophical Writings of Peirce*. New York: Dover.

Peters, M. & P. Ghiraldelli Jr (eds) 2001. *Richard Rorty: Education, Philosophy and Politics*. Lanham, MD: Rowman & Littlefield.

Posner, R. 1998. "Pragmatic Adjudication". See Dickstein (1998), 235–53.

Putnam, H. 1981. *Reason, Truth, and History*. Cambridge: Cambridge University Press.

Putnam, H. 1983. *Philosophical Papers, Vol. 3: Realism and Reason*. Cambridge: Cambridge University Press.

Putnam, H. 1987. *The Many Faces of Realism*. La Salle, IL: Open Court.

Putnam, H. 1990. *Realism with a Human Face*. Cambridge, MA: Harvard University Press.

Putnam, H. 1995a. *Pragmatism: An Open Question*. Oxford: Blackwell.

Putnam, H. 1995b. *Words and Life*, J. Conant (ed.). Cambridge, MA: Harvard University Press.

Putnam, H, 1995c. "The Question of Realism". In his *Words and Life*, J. Conant (ed.), 295–314. Cambridge, MA: Harvard University Press.

Putnam, H. 1995d. "A Comparison of Something with Something Else". In his *Words and Life*, J. Conant (ed.), 330–50. Cambridge, MA: Harvard University Press.

Putnam, H. 2000. "Richard Rorty on Reality and Justification". See Brandom (2000a), 81–7.

Putnam H. 2004. *Ethics without Ontology*. Cambridge, MA: Harvard University Press.

Putnam, H. & R. Putnam 1995a. "Dewey's Logic: Epistemology as Hypothesis". In H. Putnam, *Words and Life*, J. Conant (ed.), 198–220. Cambridge, MA: Harvard University Press.

Putnam, H. & R. Putnam 1995b. "Education for Democracy". In H. Putnam, *Words and Life*, J. Conant (ed.), 221–78. Cambridge, MA: Harvard University Press.

Putnam, R. A. (ed.) 1997. *The Cambridge Companion to William James*. Cambridge: Cambridge University Press.

Putnam, R. A. 1998. "The Moral Impulse". See Dickstein (1998), 62–71.

Quine, W. [1951] 1953a. "Two Dogmas of Empiricism". In his *From a Logical Point of View*, 3–19. Cambridge, MA: Harvard University Press.

Quine, W. 1953b. *From a Logical Point of View*. Cambridge, MA: Harvard University Press.

Quine, W. V. 1981. "The Pragmatists' Place in Empiricism". In *Pragmatism: Critical Concepts in Philosophy*, R. B. Goodman (ed.), 23–39. London: Taylor & Francis 2005.

Quine, W. 1990. "Let Me Accentuate the Positive". In *Reading Rorty*, A. Malachowski (ed.), 117–19. Oxford: Blackwell.

Ramberg, B. 2000. "Post-ontological Philosophy of Mind: Rorty versus Davidson". In *Rorty and his Critics*, R. Brandom (ed), 351–70. Oxford: Blackwell.

Ramberg, B. 2009. "Language, Mind, and Naturalism in Analytic Philosophy". See Shook & Margolis (2009), 215–31.

Ree, J. 1998. "Strenuous Unbelief". *London Review of Books* **20**(20) (15 October): 7–11

Rockwell, T. 2004. "Rorty, Putnam and the Pragmatist View of Epistemology and Metaphysics". See Malachowski (2004a), vol. 3, 141–56.

Rorty, R. 1965. "Mind–Body Identity, Privacy, and Categories". *Review of Metaphysics* **19** (September): 24–54.

Rorty, R. 1967. *The Linguistic Turn.* Chicago, IL: University of Chicago Press.

Rorty, R. 1970a. "In Defence of Eliminative Materialism". *Review of Metaphysics* **24** (September): 112–21.

Rorty, R. 1970b. "Strawson's Objectivity Argument". *Review of Metaphysics* **24** (December): 207–44.

Rorty, R. 1979. *Philosophy and the Mirror of Nature.* Princeton, NJ: Princeton University Press.

Rorty, R. 1982. *Consequences of Pragmatism.* Minneapolis, MN: University of Minnesota Press.

Rorty, R. 1984. "Solidarity or Objectivity". In *Post-analytic Philosophy*, J. Rajchman & C. West (eds), 3–19. New York: Columbia University Press.

Rorty, R. 1989. *Contingency, Irony, and Solidarity.* Cambridge: Cambridge University Press.

Rorty, R. 1991a. *Essays on Heidegger and Others.* Cambridge: Cambridge University Press.

Rorty, R. 1991b. *Objectivity, Relativism, and Truth.* Cambridge: Cambridge University Press.

Rorty, R. 1991c. "Solidarity or Objectivity". In his *Objectivity, Relativism, and Truth.* 21–34. Cambridge: Cambridge University Press.

Rorty, R. 1992. *The Linguistic Turn.* Chicago, IL: University of Chicago Press.

Rorty, R. 1998a. *Achieving Our Country: Leftist Thought in the Twentieth Century.* Cambridge, MA: Harvard University Press.

Rorty, R. 1998b. *Truth and Progress.* Cambridge: Cambridge University Press.

Rorty, R. 1998c. "Hilary Putnam and the Relativist Menace". In his *Truth and Progress*, 43–62. Cambridge: Cambridge University Press.

Rorty, R. 1998d. "Pragmatism and the Law: A Response to David Luban". See Dickstein (1998), 304–11.

Rorty, R. 2000a. *Philosophy and Social Hope.* Harmondsworth: Penguin.

Rorty, R. 2000b. "Rorty Responds". See Brandom (2000a), 87–91.

Rorty, R. 2007. *Philosophy as Cultural Politics.* Cambridge: Cambridge University Press.

Russell, B. 1945. *A History of Western Philosophy.* New York: Simon & Schuster.

Russell, B. [1908] 1966a. "William James's Conception of Truth". In his *Philosophical Essays*, 112–30. London: Allen & Unwin.

Russell, B. [1909] 1966b. "Pragmatism". In his *Philosophical Essays*, 78–111. London: Allen & Unwin.

Schiller, F. C. S. S. 1903. *Humanism: Philosophical Essays.* New York: Macmillan.

Seigfried, C. 1996. *Pragmatism and Feminism: Reweaving the Social Fabric.* Chicago, IL: University of Chicago Press.

Seigfried, C. (ed.) 2002. *Feminist Interpretations of John Dewey*. University Park, PA: Penn State University Press.

Shand, J. (ed.) 2006. *Central Works of Philosophy 5: The Twentieth Century: Quine and After*. Chesham: Acumen.

Shook, J. 2009. "F. C. S. Schiller and European Pragmatism". See Shook & Margolis (2009), 44–53.

Shook, J. & J. Margolis (eds) 2009. *A Companion to Pragmatism*. Oxford: Wiley-Blackwell.

Shustermann, R. 1999. "Dewey on Experience: Foundation or Reconstruction". In *Dewey Reconfigured*, C. Haskins & D. I. Seiple (eds), 193–219. Albany, NY: SUNY Press.

Sprigge, T. 2004. "James, Aboutness and his British Critics". See Malachowski (2004a), vol. 3, 76–92.

Sullivan, S. W. 2009. "Feminism". See Shook & Margolis (2009), 232–8.

Unger, R. 2009. *The Self Awakened: Pragmatism Unbound*. Cambridge, MA: Harvard University Press.

Voparil, C. 2006. *Richard Rorty: Politics and Vision*. Lanham, MD: Rowman & Littlefield.

Wain, K. 2001. "Richard Rorty and the End of Philosophy of Education". In *Richard Rorty: Education, Philosophy and Politics*, M. Peters & P. Ghiraldelli Jr (eds), 163–78. Lanham, MD: Rowman & Littlefield.

West, C. 1989. *The American Evasion of Philosophy*. London: Macmillan.

Westbrook, R. 1991. *John Dewey and American Democracy*. Ithaca, NY: Cornell University Press.

Westbrook, R. 1998. "Pragmatism and Democracy: Reconstructing the Logic of Dewey's Faith". See Dickstein (1998), 128–40.

Westbrook, R. 2009. "Liberal Democracy". See Shook & Margolis (2009), 290–300.

Williams, B. 1990. "Auto-da-fe: *Consequences of Pragmatism*". In *Reading Rorty*, A. Malachowski (ed.), 26–37. Oxford: Blackwell.

Wittgenstein, L. 1969. *The Blue and Brown Books*. Oxford: Blackwell.

Wolfe, A. 1998. "The Missing Pragmatic Revival in American Social Science". See Dickstein (1998), 199–206.

Wood, J. 2002. *The Broken Estate: Essays on Literature and Belief*. New York: Modern Library.

Wood, J. 2008. *How Fiction Works*. New York: Farrar, Straus & Giroux.

INDEX

157